HEALERS

The deeper impact of pet therapy

LYNNE ROBINSON

with

Rachel Brown

Copyright © 2019 by Lynne Robinson

All rights reserved. This book or any portion thereof may not be reproduced or used in any manner whatsoever without the express written permission of the author except for the use of brief quotations in a book review.

ISBN: 9781086847543

Photographs Copyright © by Ted Rosenthal/Izmaddy Studios

Library of Congress Control Number: 2019912461

www.happyselfpublisher.com

Newark, DE

Table of Contents

Introduction v

PAWS for Cancer Support *An Angel by His Side*... 1

PAWS Courthouse Companions *A Little Dog Brings a Lot of Joy*................................... 7

PAWS for Skilled Care *A Golden Boy Radiates Love and Joy*.. 11

PAWS for Drug & Alcohol Treatment *Taking Recovery Day by Day…With a Little Comic Relief*.............. 15

PAWS Trauma Support Team *Comfort in the Storm*.. 19

PAWS in the Workplace *A Charming Dog in Charm City*.. 23

PAWS for Psychiatric Support *A Tiny Dog Brings Peace and Serenity*.......................... 27

PAWS for Reading *The Story of How a Former Street Dog Gives Back*........................ 31

PAWS for Memory Loss *A Corgi Brightens Everyone's Day*.. 35

Pre-K PAWS *A Miniature Schnauzer is a Little Friend*... 39

PAWS at Hospitals *A Golden Girl Gives and Receives*... 45

PAWS at the Mobility Project *A Chocolate Chip Adds Some Sweetness*..................... 51

PAWS for Children with Behavioral Challenges *A Golden Retriever Brings Laughter and Joy*.............. 55

PAWS for Physical and Occupational Therapy *A Husky Helps with Motivation*.......... 59

PAWS Autism Initiative Program *Leaving a Legacy*... 63

PAWS for Children with Special Needs *A Goldendoodle Offers a Welcome Distraction*............. 69

PAWS to DeStress *Lightening the Load* 75

PAWS at Children's Hospitals *A Black Lab Lets Kids be Kids* 81

PAWS for Hospice *Some Final Love* 85

PAWS by Special Request *Granting Wishes* 89

PAWS at Peace *Saying Goodbye* 95

PAWS Training *A Culture of Caring* 99

Conclusion 105

To Learn More About PAWS... 107

Acknowledgments 109

About the Authors 111

Introduction

Once upon time . . . there was a big red dog. A red dog that was supposed to be a golden retriever. A big red dog who was being given up for free to whomever would take him — a four-year-old male golden retriever — good with kids — that's what the newspaper ad said. He needed rescuing, so the paper said. It turns out, though, that he was the one that did all the rescuing — and that is the story of PAWS for People in a nutshell.

But in case you'd like a few more details, here we go.

Once upon a time . . . there was a woman who needed rescuing. She had retired from teaching high school English and had tried several volunteer jobs, none of which felt meaningful or fulfilling or gave her a sense of importance or value. So she did some more exploring and ended up volunteering for her church, which was a good fit. After several years of working with church volunteers and managing the office, her pastor gave her the title of Pastoral Associate. She was happy.

But then came a giant shift in the church administration, and what was once a dream volunteer job became a nightmare. Every day became a chore, and she found she just couldn't be part of it anymore, so she made the hard, hard decision to resign — upsetting the calm life she had created after retiring. The night before her resignation meeting, she couldn't sleep; and while pacing late into the night, she realized that she had forgotten to check the newspaper for dogs up for adoption. Her only dog, Buddy, had died recently, and she was on the lookout for a new best friend. At 2:30 a.m., she found the local newspaper and saw the ad that would change her life.

It read: male golden retriever, four years old, good with kids, free. Free? Who would give away a four-year-old golden who was good with kids? Sleep came easily then, anticipation ran high, and an early phone call to the owner of this dog gave her the information she needed. The dog was still available. Her husband took off to rescue the dog, and she went to the resignation meeting — nervous, sad, and frightened. The meeting was dreadful but ended quickly. When she left the meeting room, her husband was there in the church lobby with "the golden retriever."

Boomer was leggy and tall, long-bodied, and filthy — and red. Where was the golden retriever? This dog was not what she expected. But he needed a home and seemed to be a good-natured pup. Home they went and straight to the backyard for an overdue bath. And what had started out as a muddy mess, turned out to be not only a beautiful, red-coated 115-pound golden retriever but also an immediately impressive, unusually special dog. He had an aura about him — a calming look and a gentle manner. When you looked into his deep brown eyes, you got the feeling he was looking way down deep into your very soul. It was a good feeling — thanks to this calming, warm, sentient creature. This pup was something special, and all at once, we had a double rescue going on — Boomer (whose name was soon changed to Boo Radley after a character from the novel, *To Kill a Mockingbird*) was about to save the grieving woman just as she had saved him from his abusive home.

The magic of PAWS for People began that day even though neither dog nor woman knew how their story was about to unfold.

Boo was a natural born therapy dog. His first trainer called him an "old soul" and recommended that he become a pet therapy dog, not only because of his uncanny sensitivity to people but also because of the feeling he gave everyone he met: he assured those he spent time with that he was there for them no matter what and that things were going to be okay. Part of that feeling came from his unwavering brown-eyed gaze that chased away fears and brought comfort. Part came from the warmth and kindness that naturally flowed from him to whomever he was visiting. He was exceptional. People could feel that right away. And they loved him.

Now while Boo was safe and being cared for and adored and had a job that paralleled no other, the woman was receiving everything a dog could give his person — constant acceptance, consistent love and companionship, a reminder to play, opportunities to get out and meet new people, and most importantly of all, the impact of that oh-so-powerful bond that develops between a person and her "heart dog," the dog in your life who touches your heart the most. She realized that this distinctive creature, this caring, gentle animal with the knowing eyes and subtle but insistent lean, was providing her with much needed therapy that was healing and good. And she also realized that everyone who came into contact with Boo was touched in some special way. They said they felt better, lighter, understood. They felt that through him they experienced a dose of positive therapy and felt stronger, comforted, and more at peace.

Well, if a dog could do that for her and for other people during chance meetings, then he might be able to provide the same healing love to others in a more formal pet therapy visiting situation.

Lynne, the woman, and that big red dog named Boo started visiting on their own — one visit a week to an adult day services program where they made fast friends with lots of elders needing a little human and canine attention and interaction. They visited an assisted living/dementia facility, where they learned how people with dementia might not know what day it was or who was running for political office, but they recognized Boo and called him by name when he came to visit.

They visited some severely disabled children who calmed inside and out when Boo spent time with them and became soothed and gentle, replacing the loud, uncontrolled behavior they exhibited before he arrived. It didn't seem to matter whether the people this woman and her red dog spent time with were old or young, mentally challenged or hurting, patients or staff — everyone had a positive response to this big dog, and he stole their hearts with every visit.

Lynne learned so many things from Boo and the way he treated people, the way he took time to visit with each person, and the way he had of giving something extra to each one — a lean, a gentle paw, a short rest laying on their feet. He looked into their eyes and assured them silently that everything was going to be all right — and for the time he was with them, everything was, in fact, "all right."

Lynne knew that sharing Boo was a gift she had been given — one that helped her feel better about being retired, better about what she was doing with her life, and better emotionally because of the support of this intuitive creature who had bonded so tightly with her in her pain.

Somehow visiting with Boo took her mind off the physical discomforts she was now experiencing and refocused her on life-giving things — like the joy she saw in people's eyes and the smiles she and Boo received each time they visited.

Being a joiner by nature, Lynne wanted to be part of something bigger than just her twosome, so she joined a pet therapy group in the area and became their volunteer pet therapy coordinator. This relationship lasted about 10 months, allowing Lynne to grow that group from six therapy teams and three places to visit to 141 therapy teams and 40 visiting sites. But due to some basic philosophical differences, Lynne and Boo left that group and founded their own pet therapy organization where they could focus on the things they had learned to be the most important part of pet therapy — the people being visited and the people doing the visiting. A new way of doing things evolved — a more detailed training system for the therapy teams; a "we can make it happen" approach to problem solving; and more care, support, and appreciation for the volunteers who were spending their time and sharing their pets.

PAWS for People was founded in February of 2005, and we began official visits in March. The original organization was comprised of 21 therapy teams with 10 sites to choose from. We intended to stay small and were committed to taking good care of our teams. Our mission statement grew out of recognition of the needs of our sites and the interests of the teams to underline the basic premises we believed in: PAWS teams lovingly provide elders, children, folks with disabilities, and anyone who could benefit from an individualized therapeutic visit with a gentle affectionate pet. Lynne figured that the gentle affectionate pet part was crucial, as was the loving care that the teams needed to feel when they prepared for and carried out their visits. But it is the last piece of the statement that distinguishes PAWS for People from other groups around the country — individualized, therapeutic visits. And we mean that seriously — spending unhurried time with people, one by one, and treating everyone as a friend, as an important individual, and providing them with whatever type of listening or chatting or quiet time spent with our dogs they might need — right then at that moment. Being with them where they are, accepting them however they are, and giving them time with our comforting, funny, huggable, loving therapy companions free from expectations or judgements or demands — such is the gift PAWS for People therapy teams give and surprising to most of us, the gift we receive in return.

And more people came to join us. Kind, compassionate people came with their loving, sweet dogs of every size and breed; their cuddly, purring people-friendly cats; and even their nose-twitching bunnies who could hold still enough in children's laps, helping them to focus on the content in the book as they stroke ultra-soft ears and giggle with the characters. PAWS attracted, and still does, a wide array of people who love their own pets dearly and love people just as dearly, dearly enough to invest their time into sharing the companionship and delight of their pets with people not as lucky in life as they may be.

So PAWS grew by leaps and bounds. People from the community wanted to "do" pet therapy — so we created a good solid training program to teach them the in's and out's of therapeutic visiting. That drew all kinds of folks to PAWS — moms and kids, husbands and wives, individuals coming from corporate life and non-profits, retirees and people who travel, older folks wanting to take their pets into their retirement communities, and college students sharing their pets with other students during destress sessions. And as the variety of people grew, so did the types of visits they wanted to do. Starting with eldercare and disabilities in 2005, we now offer more than 20 different types of programs that each focus on mental, emotional, and physical health across all age groups. We offer programs that range from reading sessions in libraries and schools to working with kids exhibiting behavior issues to people struggling through cancer treatments or coping with the fallout of manmade or natural disasters. The demand for our services far exceeds the capability we have in filling all the requests we receive, but PAWS tries diligently to create supportive coursework to teach our members "how to visit" whether we are asked to sit with hospice patients or incorporate our pets into occupational and physical therapy activities. We added dog training classes to our people training orientations in hopes that we could help people get their prospective therapy pets readied and well-trained enough to pass our certification evaluation, but more importantly, to feel confident and in control of themselves as a team, ready to work.

And all the time PAWS has been growing with amazingly generous people and support from the community in our increasingly varied programs, we continue to look back to what that big red dog taught us before he had to leave us in 2009 — take time to make sure each person we visit feels cared for as an individual, listen carefully and offer yourself and your therapy companion's attention to their feelings and their concerns, and make sure that everyone you meet is acknowledged and treated as a friend.

Boo could do that just by being himself. He deeply loved everyone he met, not caring about color or clothing or who those people were to the world. He was their friend and listening buddy for as long as they needed him. And watching him work — getting in close, being polite but interested always, leaving a little fur as a reminder that he had been with that person — taught me how moving, how therapeutic, how vital pet therapy can be. The impact of a good visit affects people on all levels — socially, physically, psychologically, emotionally — and the good feelings and quick rise in endorphins lasts beyond the visit, positively influencing other parts of life, giving each person something happy to remember, something interesting to talk about, and a brighter outlook on life.

AND it works! Pet therapy is an elegantly simple concept — a person, a dog (or cat or bunny), and some time. The joy of it is that it works and that it works so easily. The bond between a sweet pet and a hurting person is almost instantaneous and can be strong enough to make a little magic and do a lot of healing.

That's a lot coming from a visit with a big red golden — or a little black Chihuahua or a Great Dane or a delightful rabbit or a purring cat.

So here we are now — Pet-Assisted Visitation Volunteer Services, Inc., doing business as PAWS for People (the two "V's" make the "W" for PAWS).

We are in our fifteenth year going strong with more than 650 active therapy teams, offering more than 20 different programs in nearly 200 sites in our four-state area of Delaware, Maryland, Pennsylvania, and New Jersey. We have a board of directors, a strong infrastructure, and 10 paid employees. I remain a loyal volunteer — it's how Boo and I started and how I like it to remain. PAWS teams are doing good work and we have thousands of visiting stories to show for it. But this book has a little different purpose than to show off our stories of magic and healing.

This book is meant to share with you the goodness of pet therapy — what it can do to heal the soul, who makes the decision to volunteer their time to do this and why they keep doing it, and how important this giving process becomes in the lives of those who participate. Boo and the time spent with him visiting thousands of people changed my life in a good way. The people in this book have allowed us to get inside their own stories to learn why they share their pets and what that sharing has done for their communities, and, more importantly, for themselves.

Why do we put ourselves out there to do this work?

Please read on and meet some of the awesome PAWS people that give of their time and share their pets to create a better world for the people they visit. Each chapter describes a program and showcases a team — they all tell their own story, but the recurring theme is that the team arrives and offers comfort and joy. As the big red dog knew and taught me — spending time with our beloved pets and working together to help others magically transforms our own world into a happier place.

Lynne Robinson

PAWS for Cancer Support
An Angel by His Side

If you want to make God laugh, tell him your plans.

If this old saying is true, the Heavens must have been booming with laughter back in 2000 over Alan Burkhard's plans. That was the year he sold his multimillion dollar recruiting company in an effort to slow down and relieve some of the daily pressure he was under. "I just didn't want to have to make decisions every day," he recalled.

The sale was a success, but a few months later, the pressure had returned. This time, it was physical. "For years, I'd had spinal stenosis, but the pressure suddenly became so severe that it damaged my spinal cord," Alan explained. "At first, I had a burning sensation in my fingers, then my hand, then my whole body. The doctors told me I was very close to becoming a paraplegic."

Several surgeries spared him that fate, but Alan was left with chronic pain. Just as he was coming to grips with that new reality, he was diagnosed with a rare form of thyroid cancer. His doctors told him that he would have to undergo more surgeries and then submit to radiation; but even then, the odds were not good.

Fearing this cancer diagnosis, Alan found a natural healer who encouraged him to send out positive affirmations every second of every day. He followed this advice and learned more about meditation and ways to deal with the emotions and feelings behind chronic pain. When he went to the University of Penn Hospital to begin radiation treatments, he first had to undergo a full body scan.

"The technician looked at the screen and said, `Please report directly to the oncologist'," Alan said, remembering that he and his wife were certain it was bad news — that the cancer had spread and metastasized. "We walked down a long hallway to the oncologist's office — neither of us spoke — it felt like a death march."

Suddenly, they heard the oncologist whooping and yelling, "He's clean! He's clean!" The cancer was gone. "The oncologist came out and told us that I didn't need radiation and that I should take my wife out to lunch and get the hell out of there," Alan said, beaming. "It was the best damn hot dog and Coke I ever had."

Throughout this entire ordeal, Alan was fortunate to have Sadie, a golden retriever, at his side. "In 2000, Sadie was a puppy, so she was there for the first surgery, and she was there in 2005 through the cancer scare," he said. "My dog helped me more than all my other practitioners combined — even the surgeons — because she understood my pain."

Alan said Sadie could sense when he was in pain and knew that she had to spend more time with him on those days. "Dogs are healers," he stated. "I felt as if she took some of my pain."

Despite this firsthand experience with his own dog, Alan said he had never heard of pet therapy. That changed when he overheard a family member talking about it at a party. "I started asking her about it, and she put me in touch with Lynne Robinson who had just started PAWS for People six months earlier," he said.

Right away, he knew that Sadie would be a natural for this type of training and work. "Sadie was five by this point; and she was a sweet, kind, gentle dog — I felt she had the personality for pet therapy," he said.

When Alan and Sadie first joined PAWS, they volunteered at numerous nursing homes and adult daycare centers. "We would visit 10 to 15 sites in the area," Alan recounted. "One time, we invited everyone from the adult daycare place to come out to our farm for the day. At the end of the day, everyone loaded into the van to head back, and Sadie jumped in with them. She adored me, but she had fallen in love with this group of people. I had to climb into the back of the van and get her by the collar and haul her out."

Alan shook his head, laughing at this memory of his loving girl. They continued their work with the nursing homes and adult daycare centers, but PAWS wanted to be able to go into hospitals. "It took us years to get into Christiana Hospital," Alan stated. "It was a hard sell. The administration didn't see the value of pet therapy."

Eventually, hospital officials decided to conduct their own studies and invited PAWS to participate. "There was a heart study, and a doctor would go in and take all the vitals of a patient — heart rate, blood pressure, pulse rate," Alan explained. "And then we'd come in with a dog and have a visit. We'd leave, and the doctor would return and take the vitals again. The results were always positive."

The hospital also found that pet therapy resulted in less stress, less anxiety, and less dependency on medication, as well as better, happier patients who had shorter hospital stays. "Pet therapy is so effective that Christiana would love it if PAWS teams could come in every day for every patient," Alan stated.

Once Christiana saw the value of pet therapy, the floodgates opened and soon Alan and Sadie were making weekly visits to the Helen F. Graham Cancer Center in Newark, DE. This proved to be a natural fit for both of them. "Having had my own brush with cancer, I knew what the patients were going through more than the average person," Alan said, adding that the cancer center was a better fit than the hospital because of his own lowered immune system and compromised health. "Cancer is not contagious, so it was a good place for me to visit."

Even though Alan was well familiar with cancer and empathetic to cancer patients, he was there more to listen — a lesson he learned from Sadie. "Dogs don't talk," he said. "I tried to be quiet and let the dog be the star."

By all accounts, Sadie was the star at the cancer center (her photo was even the center's screen saver for a year). "A golden retriever is seen as a friendly dog and instantly puts everyone at ease," Alan said, remembering Sadie's soft blonde coat and her gentle brown eyes.

"The chemotherapy room holds dozens of people, and we'd walk in and the whole atmosphere would change," Alan said, explaining that people would instantly become energized. "Sadie would go to each person, and she knew when to stay, when to leave, and how to get close to people so they could pet her."

Sadie was a comfort to first-time patients who were scared of the unknown and what lie ahead; she was a comfort to the long-timers who were tired and sick from repeated infusions. Some days, she sensed that it was the doctors and staff who needed the most care and attention.

For both Alan and Sadie, it was gratifying to visit a site that had such a high impact. "There's no more upbeat place than a chemo room," he said, acknowledging that this is an astounding phenomenon. "If the patients want to live, they have to be positive."

Once people started petting Sadie, they'd start talking — to her and to one another. "People wanted to be there when Sadie was there — they were changing their appointments to fit our schedule," Alan recalled. "It was magical. The feedback was enormous — so many people told me that Sadie had made their day and made their week."

Alan also recalled going into a board meeting and seeing a man who looked familiar, but he couldn't place him. "But then he stopped the meeting and stood up and pointed to me and said: 'This man and his dog saved my life'," Alan said, remembering then that he had first seen him in the corner of the chemo room, wearing a baseball cap. "He was embarrassed to be there, and he didn't want anyone to recognize him and know he was there. But that day in the board meeting, he told me, 'As soon as your dog came over and put her head in my lap, I knew she loved me. I knew that I wasn't going to be embarrassed anymore and that I had to try to beat this'."

As heartwarming as these encounters were, Alan said the nature of this type of program means that there will be a certain amount of death and loss. "We'd come back from the winter in Florida and find out that 30 people had passed away," he said.

Still, Sadie provided a valuable service even for the terminal patients. "One woman who was there was in her late 20s, and she had a husband and two little girls," Alan said, explaining that he and Sadie spent a lot of time with family members. "We'd visit with her husband, and he'd cry and ask how he was going to manage as a single parent."

Both husband and wife struggled with how and when to tell their daughters that this was a terminal illness. "One day when we were there, the wife got on the floor and wanted Sadie on her lap," Alan said, noting that this was a 90-pound woman with a 70-pound dog. "She held Sadie and told her that she was dying. By telling Sadie, she was able to tell her girls because they were there. Everyone was crying, but Sadie never stopped looking at her."

This was a gift that Sadie was able to give this mother. "She'd never been able to say out loud to her daughters that she was dying, but she used Sadie as a vehicle to do that," Alan said.

Sadie's gift to Alan was the joy and pride of seeing her work her magic on every site visit. "It's unbelievable to see what your dog can do and how she can make someone's day," he said. "Take that incredible feeling times hundreds of site visits."

For seven years, Alan and Sadie went to the cancer center once a week, staying for an hour and a half to two hours a visit (while continuing to go to their other sites on other days of the week). "Wednesdays were our day, and Sadie would not let me out of her sight on those days — she knew the schedule," Alan stated. "It was a blessing to be able to give back with someone you love."

It was also a blessing to give Sadie such a meaningful role. "Dogs love having a purpose, and we all want that for our dogs," Alan said, pointing out that Sadie took her job seriously. "She'd come back from the cancer center and sleep for four or five hours — it took a lot out of her."

When Sadie turned 12, her big heart that had given so much to others developed a tumor, and the vet said she only had days to live. "But she held on for two months," Alan said. "It was as if she was making sure that I was okay before she could die."

Before she passed away, the center's doctors and technicians all wanted to come and visit Sadie at Alan's farm, but he knew that would be too much for his dog. In the end, it was decided that one technician would come out to visit her as a sort of representative farewell. "He brought his family, and they all sat on the porch with Sadie, petting her and telling her how much they loved her," he said. "When she died, we received dozens of bouquets of roses and hundreds of emails and notes. That was six years ago, and I still miss her to this day."

Looking back at the last two decades of his life, Alan can see now that his cancer diagnosis helped him deal with his chronic pain. "Believe it or not, it helped me to realize that it's just pain — it's not terminal," he said, adding that visits to the cancer center reinforced this message. "The pain changed me and gave me the opportunity to be a different person and understand the value of what time I have left. I'm reminded every minute of what's important."

Even though Alan's retirement plan did not include numerous surgeries and chronic pain, he has worked hard to learn his lessons and find the laughter in the tears. And even if God had a far more difficult plan for Alan, at least He sent him an angel to be at his side through the toughest times.

PAWS Courthouse Companions
A Little Dog Brings a Lot of Joy

Kathryn Meloni has a big personality — along with big hair, a big job, and a big laugh — but all of this takes a back seat to her little dog, Frangelica. And Kathryn wouldn't want it any other way. "She is my little girl, my baby," she said.

Kathryn first spotted her as a puppy on the rescue site, Petfinder. "Frangelica's ears stood straight up," she remembered. "I looked at other pictures but kept coming back to hers. She made me laugh."

The rescue group said the puppy was a Maltese/Yorkie mix and estimated she would only grow to be 10 pounds. Now seven years old, she weighs in at 20 pounds, and a later DNA test revealed that she also has strains of cairn terrier and Pomeranian. None of that fazes Kathryn because Frangelica could not be more perfect.

When she first brought her home though, the puppy was untrained and hyper. "I had her in obedience class within five days," Kathryn recalled, adding that she chose the name "Frangelica" after the hazelnut liqueur. "She was a little nutty."

The obedience trainers were impressed that Frangelica learned so quickly and had such a sweet temperament. "They were the ones who asked me to think about training her as a therapy dog," Kathryn said. When she started looking into pet therapy organizations, her mother — a longtime volunteer at Nemours A. I. duPont Hospital for Children in Wilmington, DE — told her about the PAWS teams who visited.

Kathryn and Frangelica enrolled in the PAWS training in April 2014 and have been a dedicated team ever since. Like many PAWS volunteers, Kathryn and Frangelica visit multiple sites through various PAWS programs; but as a divorce attorney, Kathryn realized the impact that pet therapy could have within the court system.

She spent a year working through the correct channels to bring pet therapy to Delaware County in Pennsylvania. "I was in touch with the county council, the district attorney's office, the dependency court, and some of the judges who are dog lovers," she explained. "I then put together a letter to the Honorable Chad F. Kenney, who was then serving as the President Judge of the Delaware County Board of Judges."

Judge Kenney appointed Judge Mary Alice Brennan and Judge Nathaniel Nichols to work with Kathryn and PAWS' staff members to bring Courthouse Companions to Delaware County. "We met with the judges and designed a program that would fit their needs," said Lynne of PAWS, adding that Kathryn has been an amazing advocate for PAWS. "Without her persistence and vision and willingness to get this going, this program wouldn't have gotten off the ground."

Kathryn estimates that it took six to eight months to get the program launched, but there are now roughly a dozen Courthouse Companions teams that visit a couple times a week at the Delaware County Court of Common Pleas that houses the dependency court (where Child and Youth Services cases are heard) and the court that handles Protection from Abuse (PFA) cases.

The courthouse is not new territory for Kathryn, but she loves going in as a PAWS volunteer. "We visit the courthouse once or twice a month and typically stay for two to three hours," she explained, adding that on any given day, there can be 80 to 160 cases at the PFA court and 10 cases at dependency court. For the PFA cases, there are victims, defendants, witnesses, attorneys, and court personnel; for the dependency cases, there are children, parents, case workers, foster parents, grandparents, and other relatives. "In both areas, that's a lot of people and a lot of bang for your buck in terms of the impact we can have."

In the waiting area inside the courthouse, Kathryn said the atmosphere is tense. "But when we first arrive, Frangelica gives a little howl that's basically her way of saying, 'I'm here! Look at me!'" she said. "It cracks everyone up."

Frangelica's elaborate dresses and hair bows probably add a little comic relief as well. Kathryn said Frangelica is excited to meet people and is very social when she first walks into the courthouse. "We'll walk back and forth to visit different groups of people," she explained, adding that she likes to show off Frangelica's tricks. "She rolls over on command, and if you say: 'Go Eagles,' she'll give you a high five. Once everyone starts to pet her, she'll lie down and become calm and relaxed."

Kathryn noted that once she's in the courthouse, she's not making judgments about plaintiffs and defendants, and that she makes it a point to visit everyone who welcomes Frangelica. "Whether you're guilty or innocent, if you're at the courthouse, you're likely having a bad day," she said, adding that her years of being a divorce attorney have helped her have a magnanimous outlook when it comes to legal disputes. "There's his story, there's her story, and somewhere in between is the truth."

The truth in this case is that petting Frangelica is a natural stress reliever in itself because she has fine, silky fur that is soothing and luxurious to the touch. Even falling asleep is a welcome interaction. "One foster grandmother was overjoyed to have her in her lap," Kathryn said. "Another little girl of three was thrilled to take her for a walk with the shorter leash that attaches to her regular leash — it was adorable."

As heartwarming as these scenes in the courthouse are, Kathryn said she's not surprised because she sees it every day in her office. "Frangelica has a bed behind my desk, and she'll greet clients and then go back to bed," she noted. "But if she hears someone getting angry or upset, she goes right to them."

Kathryn noticed this behavior about three or four months after Frangelica was certified as a pet therapy dog. "She suddenly realized that this is her role, this is her job," she said.

Being a PAWS volunteer has changed Kathryn as well. "Before, I sat on a lot of boards — you're sitting at a table making decisions," she said. "Even though many boards do a lot of good work, you don't see it; and frankly, it's a little boring. With PAWS, you see the rewards firsthand."

So Kathryn now devotes all of her volunteering time and energy to PAWS (she and Frangelica participate in two to three site visits a week through other PAWS programs). "People smile and love my little girl," she said. "Even people who are miserable light up — it's wonderful to be part of that."

PAWS for Skilled Care
A Golden Boy Radiates Love and Joy

Father Michael Szupper's room is second on the left in a quiet wing of the Oblates of Saint Frances de Sales' Annecy Hall. I gently knock on his door, which is slightly ajar, and say, "Good morning, Father Szupper, it's Denise and Roger. Would you like a visit?"

These are the words of Denise Marotta Lopes, describing her site visits to a skilled care center for elderly priests in Childs, MD. Roger is her 12-year-old golden retriever.

I wait for the sound of his voice, which is often too faint to discern. Roger knows the custom, and, at my request, sits and waits along with me. Sometimes, through the crack in the door, I see the back of the motorized recliner move as he positions himself to welcome us. After a time, I hear him indicate he's ready.

Leaving the dark hall, we enter the room. Roger instinctively knows to be calm here. I whisper, "Gently," but he already knows. Maneuvering around the black wheelchair, Roger approaches Father from the front, putting his head right near the man's hand.

"Roger Dodger! Hey, buddy. Working hard?" he asks.

Though movement is difficult for Father Szupper, he places his fingers on Roger's forehead, moving them back and forth in a gentle massaging motion. He talks to him in words I don't understand, but he and Roger seem to speak their own language.

Denise explained that Father Szupper had served as the chaplain at University of Delaware and was a beloved campus figure. "He had been very active — always running around the university grounds, palling around with the football team, setting his sheepdog loose to play with the college students when they needed a study break," she said.

Now confined to a wheelchair and in constant pain from a shoulder injury, he watches the birds outside his window. Denise follows his eyes and senses equal measures of contentment and longing and wonders if he covets the birds' freedom of movement.

I enjoy my visits with this kind man. There is a quiet strength about him. There is a television in his room, but I've never seen it on. On both sides of his chair are end tables piled with books. Often he sets down the German Bible he's been reading when we arrive. Inevitably, the conversation reverts to Roger. He tells me that Roger is like an old friend who visits. "It reconnects me with the real world."

When Roger and I visit, we bring the outdoors in. By feeling Roger's fur, Father Szupper knows if it's rained. He knows the temperature because we bring it in with us.

Denise smiles as she recalls the connection between Father Szupper and Roger. "It was so touching to see," she said. "Roger has such a gentle, kind disposition, and he's so attentive to people. Another priest who is there is much livelier, so Roger can be playful and lively himself — face to face, head in lap, tail wagging."

That face is now getting white in the muzzle (a tug on Denise's heartstrings) but still so full of love — to give and to receive. Denise and her family took in Roger as part of The Seeing Eye dog program. "We were his puppy raiser family," she explained. "We had him for a year and a half."

Roger was their third puppy that they had raised for the program — a program they viewed as a ministry — but it was an emotional wrench to part with him. "It's never easy to say goodbye, but Roger was the hardest," she recalled. "We were so attached to him; he was so attached to us."

Denise remembered worrying that he was being overtasked with long walks and sleeping in a kennel. "He always slept beside our bed," she said.

Even though Roger had passed the training for The Seeing Eye, it was proving hard to find a good match because he's such a strong dog and the fear was that he would accidentally pull a blind person down. "Because it was taking so long to match him, he started to show some anxiety so they called us and asked if we wanted him back," Denise said. "Our response was: 'Yes! When can we come and get him?' His time away from us was the longest nine months of my life."

Grinning down at her still strong and robust golden, Denise said his return to the family was meant to be. Roger, no doubt, seconds this sentiment. Even though he's getting up in years, he is clearly the baby of the family, with a large dog bed filled with toys in the living room and a daily regimen of exercises and massages posted on the fridge to keep him in top form. Denise demonstrates the 10-minute shoulder massage, and Roger closes his eyes in pleasure.

Petting Roger is a tactile treat. His fur is dense and deep, and his solid shoulders seem made to receive pats. The wide grin in the soft, kind face is its own reward. Denise remembered one Brother, who had dementia, would stroke Roger's face with both hands. "Again and again — the same motion — but Roger didn't mind," she said. "He sat still and accepted it."

Before Denise accepted a temporary position as a Teacher Associate for the fourth grade at Wilmington Friends School, she and Roger would visit the priests once a week. At first, they would stay for an hour and that soon became two hours, and then they were invited to stay for lunch. "They became like family to me — I became like family to them," she said, adding that now she visits when she can but that she looks forward to getting back to a weekly schedule once her school position comes to an end this spring.

Throughout their four years of volunteering for PAWS, Denise pointed out that the staff has been supportive and helpful from the initial training to being accessible to answer questions that arise. She has especially enjoyed learning about the value of pet therapy. "We're bringing something to people, but it's not one sided," she said. "I get just as much out of it — it's such a good feeling."

PAWS for Drug & Alcohol Treatment
Taking Recovery Day by Day…
With a Little Comic Relief

Tawanda Harbison recently celebrated her five-year anniversary as a PAWS volunteer, but this milestone pales in comparison with her journey to reach this point.

Seven years ago, Harbison was literally at death's door — a decade-long struggle with anorexia had whittled her weight down to 69 pounds, she'd lost her hair, and she'd lost her strength to the point that she could not walk.

As a last-ditch effort to give her something to live for, her parents wheeled her into a no-kill shelter run by Faithful Friends, a nonprofit animal welfare organization. There, she immediately spotted Mr. Gibbs, a puggle (half beagle, half pug), who apparently had been having his own struggles. "He was skin and bones," Tawanda said. "I was skin and bones. His ribs were showing; my ribs were showing. I remember thinking: 'This might work'."

She adopted him and knew that she had to feed him and look after him if he were going to make it. It wasn't lost on her that she had to apply the same care and feeding to herself. "At first, I'd put him on my lap, and we would go for walks around the neighborhood in the wheelchair," she explained. "As I got stronger and able to walk with a cane, he was right there at my side. He's been my buddy every step of the way."

Mr. Gibbs had a speedy recovery from his past abuse. "It really only took a few good meals — he filled out within a few weeks," Tawanda said, adding that her own recovery took almost a year.

The following year, Tawanda — who had never heard of pet therapy before — encountered PAWS for People at a community event and realized it would be a perfect fit for Mr. Gibbs. "I thought: `My dog likes people — he could do this'," she said, laughing. "He wouldn't be doing anything else — I couldn't interest him in agility competitions or anything like that."

It turns out that a kind heart was more than enough to work with folks struggling with drug and alcohol issues. Tawanda said she recently learned that her dog's former owner was prosecuted for cruelty, making Mr. Gibbs's sweet nature all the more remarkable. "He is still so loving," she said, gazing at him in slight disbelief and affection. "He's never been afraid of anyone."

Fearlessness is another useful trait for this job. Twice a week, Tawanda and Mr. Gibbs go to the Cecil County Health Department's Alcohol and Drug Recovery Center in Elkton, MD, and spend about an hour and a half at each visit. They also go to Aquilla, a substance abuse program for teenagers and young adults in Wilmington, DE. Those visits usually last two and a half hours.

In both settings, most of the people receiving treatment are there against their will. The adults in the Cecil County program range in age from 19 to their 60s and most are court-ordered to get treatment. "A lot of them are big guys who are angry," Tawanda said. "They just want to do drugs, and they don't see why it's a problem. But many of them have lost their jobs, their houses, their kids. Some of them have felony convictions."

The teenagers and 20-somethings at Aquila have not yet suffered these consequences, so they are often more aggravated at being forced to address their problems. "They have been dragged by the ear by their parents to be there, so they have an even bigger attitude," Tawanda said.

Mr. Gibbs — with his sausage-shaped body and curly tail — prances in and instantly eases tensions and lightens the mood. "Bringing a dog to this setting is about normalcy of life," explained Lynne of PAWS. "There's the outside and the inside — the dog is in the middle."

Lynne said she's seen big men with multiple piercings and tattoos pick up a dog and talk baby talk. "One man told me that this is only time he can show his feelings," she said.

Tawanda agreed that Mr. Gibbs definitely breaks the ice. "The residents see him and start talking," she said, adding that this applies to the teenagers as well. "At first, they might be standoffish and ask, 'Does he bite'?"

Mr. Gibbs is not standoffish at all. "He'll go right over and sit on someone's foot," Tawanda said.

It doesn't take long for him to go from someone's foot to sitting on the couch to cuddling up on someone's lap. From there, the group may launch into a deep conversation or may be watching an intense presentation. "Once Mr. Gibbs settles in, he'll fall asleep and then he'll start to snore," Tawanda said. "No matter what profound moment is going on, everyone will start laughing. He's his own comedy show."

Despite the comic relief of Mr. Gibbs, Tawanda said she's well aware of the pain and suffering of the residents in rehab. "The mindset behind addiction and eating disorders is not that different," she said, pointing out that maintaining health is a constant vigil in both situations. "It's day by day. It's sad to see someone leave the program and then have to come back to rehab, but it reminds me that I could backslide myself."

Still, Tawanda said she finds pet therapy deeply gratifying. "My degree is in microbiology, and I work in a lab as a researcher," she said, recognizing that this is a productive and useful profession. "But pet therapy is more rewarding."

The feedback from the staff and the residents is heartwarming. "They'll say, 'A lot of people wouldn't associate with people like us — we're so glad you come and visit'."

PAWS Trauma Support Team
Comfort in the Storm

Sue Spilecki is a serious person talking about serious subjects — natural disasters, mass shootings, suicides — and the heavy toll that these take on their victims and the first responders who are called to these scenes. At her side sits Rudy, a big chocolate Lab who clearly adores her but also looks as if he is stifling a bad case of the church giggles.

"This is what therapy pets do best in these situations — they lighten the mood," explained Lynne of PAWS.

Sue agreed, pointing out that the PAWS Trauma Support Team shows up at disaster sites to help spread the word that counselors and therapists are on hand to offer support to the victims, as well as to the first responders. In many cases, people are unaware that this help exists or they feel bad admitting that they are struggling. In both situations, pet therapy teams can break down those barriers and be the bridge to getting people the support they need.

"If I were to show up by myself and say: `Help is available,' I don't think that message would get through," Sue stated but added that showing up with Rudy changes everything. "It's an instant enthusiastic reaction — everyone wants to see him, pet him, and give him treats. Of course, Rudy is there wagging his tail and very happy to take it all in."

As part of the PAWS Trauma Support Team, Sue and Rudy have gone to schools to help students cope with tragedies like student suicides and the accidental deaths of teachers or school staff. "We'll show up with other teams and stand out front as the kids are coming into school in the morning," Sue explained. "Later, we'll be in the gym and visit with the kids as they come over by themselves or with groups of friends."

Although the teams receive psychological education as part of their training, they are not there to offer counseling themselves. Instead, they observe how everyone is reacting, and they'll alert the school guidance counselor if they see anything amiss. "The training teaches us to understand how people are impacted by tragedy and to gauge what are normal reactions to stress and grief," Sue said, adding that the training also educates the teams on what constitutes normal responses to grief among different age groups of children. "This is very useful in a school setting or an evacuation shelter because there's all age ranges there."

The pet therapy teams — and the cards they dole out to the students — also open the door to talks at home with parents. "It's not uncommon for the parents to be rattled themselves and not know what to say to their kids," Sue noted. "But if the kids are coming home and have a card about the dog who visited that day, it can launch the dinnertime conversation."

The Trauma Support Team also helps first responders deal with the aftermath of the tragedies they've witnessed. They arrived in Smyrna, DE, in February 2017 to help the employees of the Department of Corrections cope with a prison hostage situation that left one corrections officer dead. "So many of our first responders are exposed to trauma over and over again," Sue said. "Fire departments spend so much time together at the fire house that they become like a family, which is good in terms of them working as a team. But if someone's struggling, they don't want to bring in outsiders and air that dirty laundry."

For police departments, the challenge is often to get through the macho culture. "In many cases with the police, no one wants to be the first person to say, 'I need help'," Sue said.

Normally, when PAWS volunteers show up to help first responders, it's a very happy reprieve during a terrible time. "People are instantly happy to see the dogs," Sue said. "They're telling us dog stories and getting out their phones to show us photos of their dogs. Often, our visits don't go any deeper than this."

But just like with the children, the volunteers are there to observe and keep an eye out for any red flags that would indicate that someone needs help. Among adults, this could be someone who's not engaging, someone who's having trouble keeping emotions in check, someone who's being too rough with the pet therapy animal (indicating anger issues), and anyone who's behaving inappropriately (possibly a sign of using drugs or alcohol as a coping mechanism).

If the Trauma Support Team volunteers notice any of these red flags, they won't say anything to that individual, but they'll notify the crisis counselors or on-site therapists. "Then they can reach out and say: 'Let's talk'," she said.

Even though this is deeply gratifying volunteer work, Sue cautioned that it's not for everyone. "If you're the type of person who shies away from funerals, this is not for you," she said.

Sue's background as a teacher (health and physical education and driver's ed) for 21 years makes her a natural in school settings. She also said she's comfortable talking to strangers, and sadly shared that she is not a stranger herself to tragedy. "Twenty years ago, our eldest son was killed in a car accident," she said. "So we know what it's like to have your whole world up ended. Just showing up with the attitude of: 'I know you don't think you'll survive this, but you will' is a comfort."

Rudy, now the picture of health and happiness, is a survivor himself. When he was about a year old, he was picked up as a starving stray and sent to a shelter in South Carolina. "The shelters in the South are so crowded that many of them can only keep an animal five days before it's put down," Sue said. "They kept him a few days longer because he understood some basic commands so they were hoping his owners would come and reclaim him."

His photo got blasted around the Internet and showed up on Sue's computer because she had promised a coworker that she would help her look for a chocolate Lab. "Up popped that beautiful face and eyes," Sue recalled. She got in touch with the shelter and arranged to have him brought up to Delaware. The plan was that she would rehabilitate him — he had lost big patches of fur and was a scrawny 54 pounds — and then hand him over to the coworker.

"But within 24 hours, he had bonded with our yellow Lab," Sue said, adding that she could see that he met all of the rudimentary requirements for a pet therapy dog. "He's friendly, highly social, non-reactive, and easy to train because he's food motivated. In the end, I told my friend, 'I'm sorry but I'm keeping him'."

Sue had known that she wanted to volunteer for a worthwhile cause once she retired, in part, because of the role model of her late mother. "She volunteered four days a week," she said. "I knew retirement for me was not going to be about shopping and playing bridge."

To get Rudy into shape for duty, Sue set about a rigorous schedule of feeding and care. He gained nearly 40 pounds (while Sue lost 10 pounds from walking him five times a day), and his coat grew back to a beautiful glossy sheen. Sue enrolled him in two six-week sessions of obedience school and, after that, took him to PAWS for his pet therapy training. "Everything was a breeze for him except the command 'Leave it' — it's so hard for him to walk past food," she said, laughing and rubbing him on the head.

She said Rudy loves his job and often rolls over on his back to receive belly rubs. In the midst of relaying a particularly grim tragedy, Sue paused and gazed at Rudy and, with emotion in her voice, said, "Oh, I know he's just a goofy dog, but he really does make people feel better." Then she hugged Rudy and chuckled — Rudy seemed to chuckle himself, clearly devoted to Sue and appreciative of all of her love and attention — a perfect example of pet therapy in action.

PAWS in the Workplace
A Charming Dog in Charm City

There was once a young blond model who walked the runway and won award after award for his good looks and fine physique. Now, a middle-aged gentleman, those days are behind him; but, like other modern moguls, he has successfully parlayed his modeling career into corporate branding and charitable works.

Still as handsome as ever (but perhaps a little heftier), Timber, an English Labrador and former show dog, works full-time as a pet therapy dog for the Baltimore Water Taxi Co., which operates out of Fells Point in the Maryland port city.

Mike McDaniel, President and CEO of the company, has been bringing Timber to work with him ever since he adopted Timber at age two. "He was born to a breeder and was such a beautiful dog that the breeder entered him into all of these contests," he explained. Even though Timber won many of his competitions, he turned out to be sterile, so the breeder was looking for a family to adopt him.

This coincided with Mike's upcoming wedding, and his cousins wanted to give Timber as a wedding gift. "But nobody puts dogs on their registry, so they wanted my wife and me to meet

Timber ahead of time to make sure it was a good fit," he noted. "We met with the breeder who called Timber over, and he came running in and sat between us. The breeder saw that reaction and handed over his leash and food and said, `It looks like he's adopted you'."

Even though Mike is the boss at his company, he was still a little apprehensive about bringing Timber to work. "The previous owners had had corgis, and they were yappers — every time the phone rang or visitors popped into the office — everything set them off," he said, adding that this made some of his employees less than thrilled about the prospect of another office dog. "But Timber came in and introduced himself and instantly won everyone over."

Timber is not a barker or a jumper or a licker — all good traits for an office dog. But his friendly smile and outgoing personality are even bigger assets. "Right away, you could see the positive impact he was having at work," Mike said. "Everyone would take little breaks throughout the day to come over and pet him. And if he sees someone alone or off to the side, he'll come over to say hello and rub up against that person."

In addition to the pet therapy that Timber provides to the office staff and boat crew (about 80 in season; half that in off months), he is an old pro at comforting tourists in line for the water taxis. "From Memorial Day to Labor Day, we'll ferry around 150,000 to 200,000 people," Mike stated, adding that the water taxis also serve as part of the city's commuter service that runs throughout the year, and the Fell's Point location is the transfer site for those riders. "In the summer, it can be hot and people can be a little uncomfortable."

When Mike sees the lines growing long and senses frustration levels rising, he'll station Timber outside at the line to lighten the mood. "Instantly, the anxiety level decreases, and you go from a negative or neutral experience and turn it into a positive experience," he commented. "The first thing people say when they see him is: `Is he friendly?' Hearing that he's a PAWS-trained therapy dog puts people at ease. This is especially good for kids because sometimes they can be afraid of dogs."

As soon as people start to pet him, Timber lies down on the ground (easier access for belly rubs). Kids, in particular, love to stroke his ears. "He's like a huge teddy bear," Mike said, adding that he's always surprised at how many tourists already know about him. "He's a star on Instagram and social media."

To capitalize on his popularity, Stacy Steinberg, Director of Sales and Marketing and in charge of the company's social media efforts, dresses him up for all the holidays to post photos online. "She'll come out with the costume in a bag, and Timber sees it and sits perfectly still while Stacy's dressing him," Mike noted, adding that Timber knows that once he's dressed, he'll get a treat. "He's so good natured about wearing these things — hats, sunglasses, scarves — none of it fazes him."

For the month of December, Timber is dressed and posed for photos nearly every day. "It's the 25 days of Timber," Mike said, smiling and shaking his head but saying that this is a very popular posting.

Timber poses on the water taxis for photos, but only service dogs are allowed on the taxis on a regular basis, so he's not on the boats in the normal course of a day. "But Timber goes out on private charters because people request him," Mike stated, noting that these are often special events and birthdays. "For Timber's birthday, we invite six or seven dogs out on a private charter every year and have a dog birthday cake."

Timber's dog friends include the four other office dogs who have since joined the ranks. "We don't generally have five dogs in the office at the same time because some of their owners only work part-time," Mike said. "At first, it was a little chaotic, but they sorted themselves into a pack and now it all works."

Mike credited the PAWS training for providing rules and structure for having dogs in the office. "The tools they teach you help manage everyone's experience — not just the employees and visitors — but for the dogs as well," he remarked, explaining that even things like giving treats has to be spelled out. "At first, everyone who walked by wanted to give Timber treats — he got so fat, so we had to make rules about that."

In addition, Mike had baby gates installed around the office to make it easier on visitors. "If there's anyone who doesn't like dogs or who is afraid of dogs, they won't have dogs approaching them," he stated. "But most of our visitors love seeing the dogs, and now we have clients who only want to have meetings at our office because they want to see the dogs."

Local bars and restaurants are the major advertising clients for the water taxis, and they often request that Timber attend their happy hours or special events. "We bring him over and tie a balloon to his collar so we can track him as he mingles with everyone getting pets," Mike said.

As lighthearted and fun as these events are, it's important to Mike that Timber had his PAWS training and is a true pet therapy dog. As a former Marine who served 13 years and saw three combat tours, Mike continues his service to country and community and works with the American Red Cross, Team Rubicon (a veteran service organization that helps with disaster response), and the Frank J. Battaglia Signal 13 Foundation, a group that provides financial assistance to Baltimore City police department personnel in times of need. "Going forward, I'm looking into getting Timber into the PAWS Trauma Program," he said.

Timber's former life as a show dog has served him well as a PAWS dog. "If his leash gets tangled, he freezes and waits for me to straighten it out," Mike said, adding that the two-hand hold on the leash makes this a rare occurrence. "Once in a while, Timber still does his show dog walk — head held high, tail up, paws prancing — it's a sight to see."

PAWS for Psychiatric Support
A Tiny Dog Brings Peace and Serenity

Lynn Porro majored in psychology in college; she worked as a nurse for 38 years; she is a lifelong volunteer, giving her time and energy to numerous causes. No one could be more suited to visit a psychiatric unit than Lynn ... unless it's her Mi-Ki, Princess Rainy.

And no one would agree more with this sentiment than Lynn herself. "This is her calling," she said. "If she weren't a therapy dog, she would be a nun."

The little long-haired dog is calm and loving, and her serene presence is a much-needed balm in a sometimes chaotic environment. "Once Princess Rainy arrives on the scene, things settle down," Lynn said. "The patients calm down almost instantly. Even if someone is acting out, that person will quiet down and relax."

Weighing in at 3.7 pounds, Princess Rainy is the smallest PAWS animal, and this works to her advantage as a therapy dog. "She sits on laps in the day room," Lynn explained. "She can get into wheelchairs or into beds."

Patients pet her long hair and talk to her. "The psych patients love her and their visits," Lynn remarked. "They're always telling me: 'This is so much better than the medications they give us'."

Many of the patients are suffering from depression; some are undergoing electric shock therapy; others are dealing with addictions. Their doctors are trying to find the right drugs to treat their ailments, but it's not an easy process. As a result, the patients often feel really awful from all the side effects, and many feel hopeless because a new round of medications causes more side effects.

In addition to the physical discomfort, psych patients are not allowed to have their own clothes, their own shoes, or even simple possessions like a hairbrush or a picture frame. It's not uncommon for them to feel isolated and even afraid to be in with the other patients.

Having a dog visit in this setting can be greatly comforting. "This is something to hold, to love, to share feelings," Lynn said. "Patients can get down on the floor and play with the dog. It's about being normal for a little while."

A dog's natural nonjudgmental nature is an added benefit. A dog doesn't mind if someone is too quiet or too introverted. A dog is still going to provide love and total acceptance.

Princess Rainy embodies that love and acceptance, and it also helps that she has a mellow temperament. "Nothing rattles her," Lynn pointed out, noting that she's not prone to barking or sudden moves. "This is important because sometimes patients have tubes or medical equipment attached. She can nestle in and not disturb anything."

Lynn and Princess Rainy visit the psychiatric unit at Christiana Care Wilmington Hospital once a week and stay for 20 minutes to an hour. "It depends on the volume of patients and how many people are in the day room," Lynn said, adding that they've been PAWS volunteers for the past eight and a half years.

Not everyone is enthusiastic to see a dog, but Lynn noted that she never pushes Princess Rainy on patients. "But even the people who initially say they don't like dogs often come around," she observed. "Once she's been around the room, that same person will be saying, 'Oh, can I see her'?"

Lynn smiles when she thinks of Princess Rainy's most enthusiastic fans on the psych ward. "The staff loves her," she said. "This is a stressful job for them, so a dog visit is a comfort to them as well."

The affection is mutual. "That dog is having a love affair with the group facilitator," Lynn said, laughing. Perhaps he's the reason Princess Rainy dresses up to go on site visits. She owns more than 40 dresses and loves wearing them.

"At home, she likes to lie on the couch all day because it's the perfect spot to look into the backyard," Lynn said. "But when I get out a dress, that's her cue that she's going on a visit, and she'll run to the door."

Princess Rainy is one of nine dogs in her somewhat loud but joyful home. "She loves to go in the car and have me to herself," Lynn said. "After our visit, we go to Rita's and she gets a small vanilla custard — that's our ritual and it's her reward."

Lynn recalled that finding Princess Rainy was a lucky accident. "I was looking up an antibiotic, methicillen, and the first page that popped up online was a page about Mi-Kis," she said. "I knew that was the breed for me."

She soon discovered that the nearest breeder was in Pennsylvania, so she called. "The woman told me that they were packing up and moving to Florida but promised to stop on their way down to show me a puppy," Lynn said, adding that it was such a rainy summer, that she'd already decided on the name, Rainy. "I still remember seeing her for the first time. Our eyes met and it was love at first sight — I also knew I would add `Princess' to her name."

Almost instantly, Lynn realized what a special dog she had and went back online to find an organization for pet therapy. "I found Lynne and PAWS for People, and that was that — we started when Princess Rainy was only five months old," she said.

Lynne of PAWS remarked that Lynn's dedication is admirable, especially given that she has chronic pain from fibromyalgia and shoulder surgery. "Through all of this, she's still made her round of visits," Lynne said. "In many ways, these serve as a respite from her own problems."

In addition to a wonderful dog and meaningful volunteer work, Lynn is grateful for the many friends she's made within the group, with Lynne Robinson at the top of the list. "We clicked instantly and started going out for tea and coffee," she said. "Lynne and I are a good support system for each other and can share moments in life that are happy and sad. You know dog people are good people."

PAWS for Reading
The Story of How a Former Street Dog Gives Back

One look at Birch's earnest expressive face and it's clear that he's saying, "Yes? Do you have something you want to tell me?" This — along with his love of children — makes him the ideal canine volunteer for PAWS for Reading.

For the past 11 years, Karen Brubaker and Birch have been making the rounds at local schools and libraries to help struggling readers improve their skills. "The child will put a quilt or blanket down on the floor and get cozy," Karen explained. "Birch usually lies down, and the child can snuggle in close or sit apart."

The children pet Birch, and he looks attentively at the pictures in the books that are being read. "If a child struggles with a word, sometimes I'll lean in and ask, 'Can Birch help? Birch thinks that word is _____'," Karen remarked.

It's not uncommon for poor readers to whisper as they read out loud. In those cases, Karen will say, "Birch can't hear you — can you speak up a little?"

Over the years, Karen noted that she's seen so many children make progress and become confident and strong readers. Children with poor reading skills are often reluctant to read out loud and sometimes can be defiant about it, telling their teachers or parents: "I'm not going to read."

The dog is a bridge to these difficulties. "The dog radiates acceptance and calmness and conveys, 'I'll sit with you'." she said. "The child thinks, 'The dog isn't going to make fun of me if I stumble over a word'."

Karen worked for 40 years as a school counselor and came to love middle schoolers, so she chooses to visit 6th, 7th, and 8th graders at Radnor Middle School in Wayne, PA, and Springer Middle School in North Wilmington, DE, adding that working with this age group is challenging but deeply rewarding.

"By this age — 11, 12, and 13 — it's debilitating to be behind in reading," she explained. "This group very much wants to fit in with their peers, and they don't want to read aloud and be exposed for lagging behind."

But even difficult tweens are willing to read in front of a dog. "They think it's cool," Karen said, smiling at their reactions when she and Birch go into school. "You see it in their faces when we arrive. They are so excited to see Birch."

When Birch first spies children — or even hears their voices — he gets up on his hind legs to get a better look. His other big "trick" is his "drop and roll," which he performs to get belly rubs.

Karen and Birch spend a few hours at both schools (twice a month at Springer; once a month at Radnor). "Because we're not there every day, they have to tell Birch what has happened in the story," Karen said. "This means they have to have a sense of sequence, recall, and expression — all important skills."

At the Brandywine Hundred Library in Wilmington, DE, Karen brings Birch in for one hour visits twice a month because the librarians have scheduled children (generally Kindergartners through 5th graders) for 15-minute reading intervals. A recently immigrated family from Russia comes in every week to help their daughters learn English. "They miss their dog back in Russia so they love seeing Birch, and their father insists that they speak to him in English," she said.

The library also hosts a social group for developmentally delayed adults. "One man comes in with his brother every week and reads Birch a Dr. Seuss book," she said. "He's become more confident with his reading and with people."

Another boy on the autism spectrum has been coming to the library for two years and has made huge strides. "When he first started coming to the library, he was very quiet, wouldn't look at Birch, and was not interested in reading," Karen stated. "But now he's much more confident, and his reading is much improved. He'll look and talk to Birch and even to me a little. He's no longer having homework problems, and he reads to his own dog at home. His mother attributes all of this to PAWS and to Birch."

At 18 (over 100 in dog years), Birch is one of the oldest PAWS volunteers, but he remains spry and ready to dash out to the car when it's time to visit a school or library. Karen credits his longevity and robust health with being a "marvelous mutt" and jokingly refers to him as a "Puerto Rican street dog."

Although this isn't an actual breed, Birch was rescued along with a Dalmatian by a military man who was stationed in Puerto Rico. When he returned home to New Jersey, his family decided to keep the Dalmatian and put the smaller, cuter dog up for adoption. An Army sergeant took him but then was quickly deployed overseas, so she placed him in a Sheltie Rescue, which is where Karen found him.

Birch somewhat resembles a Sheltie, but Karen paid for a DNA test and discovered he's actually a mix of six different breeds (not a Sheltie in the mix). "I've had dogs my whole life, but this is the most marvelous dog I've ever had," she commented, adding that she named him "Birch" because his brindle-colored top coat and creamy underbelly reminded her of the colors of birch beer.

Karen's vet estimated that Birch was two or three by the time Karen adopted him, but she was shocked at how much he had to learn to become domesticated. "Birch was a feral dog, so he didn't know what it was to be inside, to have his own bed, to have people around," she said. "It took him a year and a half to accept that he would be fed every day and didn't have to hoard dog treats."

All that care, feeding, and training has proven to be a huge investment in a small sweet dog who constantly gives back.

PAWS for Memory Loss
A Corgi Brightens Everyone's Day

"Hi — we're with PAWS for People. Would you like a visit today?" This is the greeting that Christina Summa uses as she walks the halls of the memory loss wing at Country House, a retirement community in Wilmington. Accompanying her is Jax, a tri-color (black, white, and tan) corgi. Specifically, he's a Pembroke Welsh corgi, so that means he has no tail, but that doesn't slow him down as he happily trots along making the rounds.

The two of them are a perfect match in looks and disposition — Christina is young and pretty, and Jax is a handsome ham — they both walk in, smiling and making eye contact. Jax instantly sidles up against a resident's legs — whether standing, sitting, or in a wheelchair — and is ready to receive pets and compliments. If a resident is lying down, Christina picks Jax up, making it possible to give a pat or to get a better look.

Christina makes it a point to get on the same level as the resident so she often kneels down if someone is sitting. Because so many of the residents are hard of hearing, she naturally raises her voice, but her constant smile makes it clear that this is a pleasant exchange.

In the hour or so that she and Jax are there (they usually visit twice a month), Christina will answer questions about Jax:

"Yes, a corgi, just like Queen Elizabeth's dogs."

"He does consider himself royalty."

"Jax is three years old."

"Yes, he loves being scratched behind his ears."

She also asks an ideal mix of past and present questions to the residents:

"Is this your family in this picture?"

"What did you have for lunch today? Was it good?"

'What's on TV? A movie about golf — are you a golfer?"

"This is a nice view from your window — do you like to watch the birds?"

"Where did you grow up? In Milford — did you go to the beach often?"

The visits themselves can be long or short, and Christina seems to sense when someone wants her and Jax to stay a little longer. One resident was delighted to see Jax and sang him several songs (it's very easy to guess that these were songs she sang to her own babies and grandchildren). Jax loved being sung to and grinned the whole time. Another resident showered him with kisses and pets and spoke to him in Polish; he agreed wholeheartedly with whatever was being said to him.

Christina explained that she grew up with corgis and realized how much she missed having a dog once she was out on her own. When she adopted Jax (named after the main character in *Sons of Anarchy*), she realized how smart he was. "He's very good at listening, so I knew he would be easily trained," she said, adding that his love for attention and for her grandparents made him a good candidate for pet therapy. Her own close relationship with her grandparents is probably what makes Christina a natural with older people. Also, her grandmother suffers from Alzheimer's but still loves visiting with Jax.

Jax received his PAWS certification when he was a year old, and they've been volunteering for two years. "Jax considers this his job," Christina said, adding that her job is as a commercial real estate analyst with a bank. "He's very excited when he sees me get out his PAWS leash — he wants to come here and spend time with everyone."

This is surely a two-way sentiment. "Everyone wants to pet him," Christina commented. "The residents are excited to see him — it makes them feel good to have a visit."

Pre-K PAWS
A Miniature Schnauzer is a Little Friend

🎵Walky walkies ... walky walky walky ... walky walkies ... walky walky walky 🎵

Imagine these words sung happily to the tune of the French nursery song, "Alouette." This is what the four and five-year-olds of the University of Delaware Lab Preschool in Newark, DE, sang to Zenny, a miniature Schnauzer, as they took turns walking him around the playground. Hard to say which Zenny enjoyed more — the walking or the singing — but he was certainly enjoying his time with the preschoolers.

Also hard to say was whether it was Zenny or his owner, Marilyn Huebner, who was enjoying the site visit more. As a retired Kindergarten teacher, it's apparent that Marilyn loves this age group and has a natural rapport with them. Go one step further in and it's equally hard to say if it were the children who enjoyed this PAWS visit the most.

Their faces lit up when they first spotted Zenny, and they all smiled and waved, "Hi Zenny ... Look — it's Zenny ... Hi Zenny." They immediately turned to Marilyn and asked, "Where's

Molly Bear?" Marilyn told them that Molly Bear (her golden doodle and longtime PAWS dog) was home because it was Zenny's turn to be with them.

While Molly Bear and Marilyn have been PAWS volunteers for more than five years, Marilyn held out little hope that Zenny could be a PAWS dog. "I named him Zenny, hoping he would become more Zen-like," she said, noting that he was a hyper puppy and not good at listening.

She also shared that she knew practically nothing about miniature Schnauzers when she first got him. "A friend of mine had children who were highly allergic to most dogs, so she researched this breed and discovered that they have minimal shedding and dander," Marilyn explained, adding that the friend invited her to go to the breeder. "We got there, and there were three puppies. She picked up her two for adoption, and I asked the breeder what would happen to the third puppy. She told me that he would go back in the crate."

Marilyn could not bear the thought of the lone puppy going back into the crate without his cousins, so she adopted him on the spot. She figured he would be good company for Molly Bear, even if he weren't suitable as a pet therapy dog.

"But the folks at the PAWS office kept urging me to put him through the training, so I finally did — mainly just to show them how he wouldn't pass the certification test — and, of course, he proved me wrong and was perfect and even passed the advanced test," she said.

Back on the playground, Nora Jacobson informed Marilyn that her birthday was in two days and she would be five. Marilyn was delighted to hear this happy news and suggested that the birthday girl should be the first to walk Zenny. They attached a shorter leash to his collar (Marilyn still held the longer leash), and they set off around the playground with a small group of children who wanted to join the dog walk.

It was a rainy day, and Nora asked Marilyn if Zenny has little dog boots. Marilyn told her that he does. "But he hates wearing them," she noted. "He takes them off with his teeth."

This produced a squeal of giggles from the little group, and then Nora asked, "Can you put those on him again — I would like to see that."

When Master Teacher Monica Shire heard about the boot exchange, she laughed and said she was not surprised, "Nora is our fashionista."

After a short stroll, Nora handed the leash over to the next preschooler. When other little ones announced that they would like to walk Zenny, Marilyn assured them that they'd all get a chance, but they must take turns. "Learning to take turns is a big lesson in preschool," Marilyn commented.

Monica pointed out that this is one of the many lessons that a PAWS visit imparts. "Children are sometimes socialized to be afraid of dogs," she said, adding that not only does a pet therapy visit acclimate children to dogs, it also teaches them how to be safe around dogs. "We teach them that they have to ask first if it's okay to pet the dog. They learn how to walk a dog; they learn that dogs have feelings — that they can be good listeners and good buddies. They learn how to give treats."

Marilyn reinforced all of these lessons. At one point on the dog walk, she stopped and asked the children, "Should we pet Zenny and tell him what a good boy he is and that he's doing a good job?" They agreed and showered him with pets — and a few treats — Zenny was a willing recipient.

The PAWS visits also help preschoolers learn to be gentle. "On a previous visit, one boy was being too rough, but the other children ran over and interceded," Marilyn said. "They learn that they can't pet too hard — they'll police themselves."

Monica noted that Zenny models gentleness himself. "He's a calm, sweet dog," she stated, admitting that she's an avid dog lover herself with a Pekingese/poodle mix at home. "We have a class guinea pig, but the children don't pay much attention to him. Dogs are so much more relatable."

When the children tromped in from the playground and returned to their classroom, Monica put on some music, and they all did a rousing performance of the bean bag dance. Marilyn laughed and clapped her hands to the beat. Zenny was in her lap, but he was more focused on the guinea pig (at least someone finds him of interest).

Next, it was circle time, and Marilyn led Zenny into the middle of the play area on the floor. Zenny was now the center of attention, and Marilyn showed the children his whole lineup of tricks — roll over, catch, crawl, and dance — the children laughed and clapped for Zenny. Preschooler Layaan Quazi asked, "Does he juggle?" The grownups cracked up over this question, and Marilyn told her that maybe they'll start practicing.

The rain held off long enough to take a walk over to the James H. Hall trail, which runs behind the school property. After a short walk through a grass field, the children hit the trail and ran to a bridge. Zenny's ears perked up and he was ready to run himself. Preschooler Marco Munzo had asked to hold Marilyn's hand, so they walked and brought up the caboose.

The bridge spans a small creek, and the children were soon happily splashing in the water. Preschooler Luis Rayon-Reyes asked Marilyn if Zenny likes to jump in puddles, and she replied that he's sometimes a little hesitant about water. Still, Zenny was there to watch and receive pets. At one point, Luis reached over to pat Marco's head and said, "Look, I'm petting you, Marco."

Marco laughed and told him, "I am not the doggie." Marco asked Marilyn how she can tell what Zenny is saying because he doesn't talk.

Marilyn explained that she can sense things with Zenny. "I know when he's happy because he's smiling; I know when he's scared — like during a thunder storm — because he's shaking," she said.

Even though the children encouraged Zenny to get into the creek, he kept a watchful distance. Towards the end of their time though, Zenny decided he would like to get closer, so Marilyn walked with him to the edge of the creek. Finally, with just a few minutes of outdoor time left, Zenny got into the water with the children.

Preschooler Finley Fongeallaz was in the creek beside him and was especially pleased to see that Zenny decided to join them. Marilyn told her that Zenny probably worked up his confidence to get into the water after watching her and the other children. Finley nodded solemnly and said, "He just needed a little bit of time."

Marilyn and Zenny (or Molly Bear — they alternate) visit the preschool every other Friday during the school year and typically stay for an hour or two. Monica stated that PAWS has been coming to the preschool for the past four years.

"We appreciate PAWS and their dedicated volunteers, who donate their time to children and animals," Monica stated, with Marilyn adding in how much she loves these visits herself.

Monica grinned and said, "It's win, win, win."

PAWS at Hospitals
A Golden Girl Gives and Receives

It's not uncommon for PAWS volunteers to participate in multiple programs. For many, it's a mix of logistics and interests in that they may live near a local library or school or they were already visiting a family member or friend at a particular facility.

When Mary Perno first started volunteering with PAWS with her golden retriever, Abby, they were going to a nursing home. "Nearly everyone there had dementia, so they enjoyed our visits, but no one ever remembered us," she said, adding that the exception was one woman who had a brain tumor. "We would visit with Sandy for three or four hours at a time and sit and talk with her because she was lonely there."

Over time, Sandy became progressively worse. One day, Mary and Abby arrived at the nursing home and started down the hallway to her room. "All of sudden, Abby put the brakes on and refused to move," Mary recalled. "But then one of the nurses walked by and said she was sorry to tell me that Sandy had died. Abby knew it before she'd said a word."

Abby couldn't be coaxed down that hallway that day, nor in the days or weeks that followed. "Since so many of the nursing home residents were off limits because their rooms were down that hallway, we switched over to Christiana Hospital," Mary said, noting that she chose the hospital in Newark, DE, because it's such a large facility. "I knew we could cover a lot of ground there, especially since Abby could work for four or five hours straight."

Even though Mary had a full-time job at the time running the substance abuse program for the University of Delaware's Center for Alcohol and Drug Studies, she and Abby would go to the hospital twice a week. They did this for 11 years.

Looking back at their time there, Mary has many fond memories and is grateful for all they were able to do there. "Abby was the first dog allowed in the emergency department," she said. "We'd spend two or three hours at a time there — in the halls, in the waiting rooms, visiting patients and their families."

Another first was in the intensive care unit (ICU), where a woman in her 60s was recovering from a stroke. "Her daughter approached us in the lobby and asked if we'd go see her mom," Mary said. They entered the room and saw that the woman could not move — the stroke had completely paralyzed her.

"We put Abby into her bed so she could lay next to her," Mary explained. "We went to visit her every two days. Eventually, she could move a finger, and then she progressed to being able to use her hand to pet Abby. Later, she was able to brush her."

When she was able to get out of bed and start walking, Abby was there to walk beside her. "The doctors and nurses could not believe it," Mary stated. "They'd come and say, 'We need to witness this for ourselves.' This took weeks and weeks, but we helped her get back from having no movement at all to taking a walk."

After that, Abby had many more requests to go to the ICU, and Mary said she never said no to a request. One of her favorite requests came from labor and delivery — from the wife of the hospital's vice president. "We showed up right after the baby was born," she remembered, laughing at the fact that this baby just turned three. "We were their first visitors, and they were taking pictures of us and saying they wanted them for the baby book."

Another special request took them to a hospital in Wilmington because one of the Christiana nurses was having knee surgery there and wanted her own visit from Abby. Mary found this funny because this same nurse once had been deathly afraid of Abby. "The first time she saw her, she stood up on her chair and was yelling, 'Dog! Dog! Dog'!" she said, explaining that this nurse had been bitten by a dog as a child.

In time, Abby won her over. "All the nurses loved Abby, but this nurse adored her — she'd buy her treats, she'd be on the floor with both arms around her, she brought her little cups of crushed ice," Mary recounted.

Abby was a big hit with the patients as well. As an average-sized golden, she was the perfect height for hospital beds. She had a shorter coat than most goldens, but Mary reported that everyone commented on how soft and silky it was to the touch (thanks to weekly baths). Abby also was more red than blonde. "She's a gorgeous redhead," Mary said, adding that her bushy tail adds to her look. "That red tail makes her look like a fox."

Mary marvels at Abby's sweet nature because the tattoo on her stomach suggests that she was a rescue from a puppy mill. "I got her when she was about 15 months old, and the vet said she'd already been through two pregnancies," she noted.

Despite her hardscrabble start in life, Abby was determined to soak up all the good that Mary — and her friends at Christiana — were doling out. "She knew who gave the best head rubs, the best belly rubs, the best backside scratches," Mary remembered. "I would tell people: 'This dog has scheduled a full-body massage for today'."

All of this attention made Abby love going to the hospital and seeing the patients. "She was happy, happy, happy to be there," Mary said. "She'd walk in and shake hands like she was the mayor."

Even though Abby was empathetic to individual patients and could sense their emotions, Mary was relieved to see that her sweet dog did not take in their pain. "She could feel what they were feeling, but she didn't hold that in and retain that tension and anxiety — she would be just as happy going in to visit the next person," she stated.

This ability to "empathize and release" as Mary calls it was essential for both of them. "My daughters are both in medicine, and they taught me that I could not dwell on each and every patient's problems because that would make me depressed — and depressing — to all the patients," she said, adding that it wasn't uncommon for Abby and her to visit 100 patients during a visit (and registering five miles on her Fitbit).

Mary also observed that if she allowed herself to feel everyone's pain and sorrow, Abby would sense this in her and be affected. "Both of us always wanted to enter each patient's room with upbeat vibes," she said. "They were having a tough enough day on their own that they didn't need to feel like they had to cheer us up."

In the fall of 2015, Mary and her family moved to North Carolina and soon began volunteering at a local hospital down there. That particular hospital only allowed two-hour visits, but that suited Abby, since she was getting older and slowing down.

The following fall, Mary was the one who sensed something was up with Abby. "One day, we were in the hospital and had a list of 30 patients to visit," she explained. "But Abby wasn't walking with me. She lay down on the floor and her tail stopped wagging. I didn't know what was wrong, but I knew this wasn't Abby."

The next patient they went to see had met Abby two or three times before. "She took one look at her and said, 'What's wrong with Abby'?" Mary recalled. "That confirmed it, and we went to see the vet that day."

The vet gave Mary the sad news that Abby has lymphoma, a cancer of the immune system. This diagnosis means that Abby's days will be coming to an end sooner than expected; but it also heralded her retirement because the medications make her ill, and it's difficult to transport her. Mary said she's hidden Abby's green scarf and PAWS leash because it would be too heartbreaking to let her see these and get her hopes up that she can go back to the hospital.

Mary continues to love her golden girl and vows to cherish the time they have left together. Shortly after Abby's retirement, they both had a heartwarming surprise. "The folks from the hospital called and said they'd heard Abby was sick and couldn't come anymore," Mary said. "They asked if they could come visit her."

Mary assured them that Abby would love visits. "The hospital administrators and the other volunteers come to the house and pet her and love her and hang out," she said. "Abby loves it. Instead of PAWS for People, it's the reverse — it's People for PAWS."

PAWS at the Mobility Project
A Chocolate Chip Adds Some Sweetness

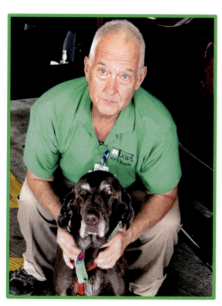

Rick Altemus beams with pride as he shows off an entire wall of framed newspaper articles and certificates all relating to his chocolate Labrador, Chip. Chip is at his side and senses he is saying glowing things about her — she hangs her head with a humble "Aw shucks" look on her face but wags her tail in sly delight.

There's no question that Chip is an accomplished and print-worthy dog, but Rick himself could easily have his own wall of accolades. Nine years ago when he handed his carpentry business over to his adult sons and went into semi-retirement, he was casting around for something to do with his free time. "At the time, my wife, Ann, was taking her sister-in-law to the Helen F. Graham Cancer Center for treatments and saw a PAWS dog there," he said. "She suggested I do this."

Over the years, Rick and Chip have participated in a wide variety of PAWS programs. But Lynne of PAWS pointed out that his carpentry skills came into the most use during his two years at the University of Delaware's Mobility Project, a program designed to foster movement for young children born with developmental disabilities, such as spina bifida and multiple sclerosis. The program, founded in 2000 by Dr. Cole Galloway, is now called GoBabyGo and has chapters all over the country.

"We'd go in every week for an hour visit," Rick said, adding that he always made sure to arrive early. "As soon as we walked into the building, kids wanted to pet Chip; the staff wanted to pet her. Some days, it took us 20 minutes to get where we needed to go."

Most of the children in the program were there as the result of congenital conditions (versus accidents), but he was respectful of the health privacy laws and did not ask for specifics. Instead, he focused on what the staff was trying to accomplish with each child. "Every time we went in there, I'd ask: 'What are you working on today'?" he said, adding that the staff was wonderful at incorporating Chip into their sessions.

One of Rick's favorite memories of his time with this program was how he and Chip helped a four-year-old boy. "The little guy had cerebral palsy and was in a wheelchair," he said. "He had no movement in his body except for between his elbow and hand — even his fingers were in a fist. The therapists wanted to expand on that range of motion."

Putting his carpentry skills to work, Rick built a little tray table with a hole in it and a curved chute; he rigged it so the little boy could throw Chip a ball. "This helped him work on his motor skills, and the reward was seeing Chip chase after it," Rick explained, adding that the device could throw the ball 15 to 20 feet. "It's no fun if it just plops off the wheelchair onto the floor."

This ball-shooting device didn't work the first time, and Rick had to go back to his shop and make adjustments (with a little help from PVC piping). He soon discovered that he also had to make adjustments and tweaks to how he handled and trained Chip for this environment.

For example, Rick taught Chip to obey verbal commands from everybody and also taught her hand signal commands. "The children could say a command like 'Sit,' and Chip would sit — they wouldn't see me doing the hand signal," he said. "It really gave the kids a huge bump of self-esteem and self-worth to see Chip respond to their commands."

PAWS training reinforced basic pet therapy practices like "Leave it," which is especially important in a medical setting. "Things fall on the floor — toys or even medications — and it's a safety issue that your dog not touch them," Rick stated.

For this setting, Rick also taught Chip not to turn around if someone touched her tail. "That's a big deal because kids would tug on her tail," he said, adding that he also taught Chip to back up versus turning around. "I didn't want her to bump into equipment or knock out IVs."

Pet therapy dogs must be well groomed to receive pets and be sanitary in their environment. Rick encouraged the children to participate in Chip's care. "I always brought in soft brushes to let the kids brush Chip," he noted. "I brought in tooth brushes and let the kids brush her teeth."

Chip remained calm and unruffled through these sessions. "She would lay on the floor and the kids would crawl on her," Rick stated. "She would stand still as a child would balance against her to step onto a bench. A child unable to stand on his own could lean on Chip's back."

The therapists at the Mobility Project would also have Chip walk 10 feet in front of a child in a wheelchair. "It was the child's job to follow Chip and maneuver around cones," Rick explained.

Chip was especially useful as a distraction from the pain and discomfort of physical therapy, particularly when the therapists would be working on the kids' hips and legs. "It was agony for the kids," Rick said, pointing out that having a dog there really helped. "Part of it was the novelty of a dog, especially for the kids who didn't have a dog at home. Also, adults are not down at their level, but a dog is, so that is instantly a friend."

Chip's love of children proved to be a huge asset in this arena. "She's been a love bug from day one," Rick said, smiling at his old friend. "She would always give the kids a kiss, would always wag her tail. To see the kids smile was a fantastic feeling."

Eventually, it was Rick's own decreased mobility (following back, knee, and ankle surgeries) that led him to move on from his work at the Mobility Project. "I couldn't risk being unstable around the kids, and my schedule was causing me to miss too many days and to be inconsistent," he said. "Repetition and routine is so important to this group, so I couldn't do that to them."

But Rick is still very much active in PAWS, going out on five visits a week to a rotating 30 sites in various programs. Chip is now 10 and has torn a ligament in her leg, requiring surgery and physical therapy herself. When she was going through that, Molly — Rick's six-year-old shih tzu/poodle mix — stepped in to handle Chip's visits and is still a regular participant. "She's my backup quarterback," Rick stated.

Rick and his wife spend their winters in Florida, and as much as they enjoy getting away from the snow and cold weather, Rick said he and Chip both miss their volunteer work when they're away. "PAWS is really about community and giving back," he said.

Rick fosters community and gives back himself by organizing and sponsoring a fundraiser every year in Chesapeake City, MD, giving a portion of the proceeds to PAWS. "My son, Eric, died in 2012, and his brothers wanted to do something in his memory," Rick said. "Eric loved to fish, so we decided to hold a catfish competition. The first year, we had a little more than 100 people participate; but in the last two years, we've had between 325 and 350 people here."

The pain from the surgeries and the mental suffering of losing a child prompted Rick to get Chip certified as a service dog. "She helps me both physically and mentally," he said. "And going out on all of these site visits every week greatly helps with my depression."

Although Rick initially joined PAWS as a way to spend some of his free time in retirement, his journey throughout the past nine years has not been easy. By many accounts, Rick could easily be a candidate to receive pet therapy; but, instead, he's out there giving back and finding healing and strength in that role. Surely, that dedication to service and community deserves its own spot on his wall of fame.

PAWS for Children with Behavioral Challenges

A Golden Retriever Brings Laughter and Joy

It is late afternoon on a Friday the 13th. The calendar says it's spring, but there's a chill in the air. Laurie Napolin pulls into the parking lot of the New Castle County Detention Center in Wilmington, DE, a juvenile correction facility. Before heading into the squat brick building, she takes a deep breath, straightens her shoulders, and resigns herself to the fact that there's no telling how things will go.

Once inside, she stops at the security front desk to hand over her car keys, her phone, and opens her purse and tote bag for inspection. She then walks through a metal detector and the first set of reinforced locked doors — a guard swipes an ID card at each door to open it. The halls are glassed in and feel eerily still — footsteps echo. Finally, at the last set of doors, Laurie is in a small gym.

Almost immediately, three young men — ranging in age from 12 to 14 — arrive on the scene. They beeline over to her — or rather to her five-year-old golden retriever, Scout. "Hey Scout — remember me? How's it going? Give me a paw."

Okay, okay ... despite the date and the location, this is not a horror movie because horror movies don't feature golden retrievers and certainly not one as sweet and lovable as Scout.

Scout is overjoyed — and has been ever since Laurie tied on his green PAWS bandana and put him in the car — and greets the boys with a big smile, nonstop wagging tail, and, of course, gives his paw. Within minutes, Laurie is digging into her tote bag and giving the boys a tennis ball to toss against the gym walls. "This is wall ball — they all love this," she said, referring to the boys and the dog.

Laughter reverberates around the gym, and Laurie soon digs into the tote bag again and hands the boys a chewed up football. They immediately launch into a monkey-in-the-middle game, with Scout as the monkey. He is such an active, enthusiastic participant in all the games that it's easy to imagine him as a little boy who's been allowed to hang with the big kids.

Laurie reinforces this image by sharing that one time the boys came in and were more interested in shooting hoops and playing with one another than they were with playing with Scout. "I told them they couldn't ignore him — this was for him as well," she said.

There's no lack of attention for Scout at this visit. Laurie doles out a handful of goldfish crackers to the boys for a game of hide and go seek. The boys scatter to hide these treats around the gym while Scout sits with Laurie, supposedly with his back to the boys. But he keeps sneaking peeks, making the boys laugh and yell (and re-hide the treats). "Scout! You're cheating!" Laurie exclaims, getting more laughs from the boys and a shrug from Scout. He soon sets off around the gym to find the hidden crackers.

Next, there's a footrace from one wall of the gym to the next and then back. The boys and Scout line up; and, at the count, they all start running. The boys run to the other wall, but Scout only runs halfway and turns to run back to the starting wall. "Miss Laurie, Scout's cheating again," the boys yell.

"Oh, Scout — that's too much," Laurie tells him as she pats him on the head. "You can't win like that." Everyone laughs.

All this activity is tiring for Scout. When he lies down to take a little break, this is Laurie's cue to get out the dog comb and let the boys groom him. She reminds them that he doesn't like to have his tail brushed. One boy asks for his water dish and takes it to the water fountain to fill it up for him. Aimee Elson, the Volunteer Service Coordinator for the center, observed that these activities allow the boys to be nurturing and empathetic. "It's good for them to take care of something," she said.

Even after his grooming and water break, Scout is panting a little bit. Laurie asks the boys if they know why dogs pant. They offer some ideas, and Laurie explains that dogs don't have sweat glands and that panting serves the same function for dogs as sweating does for humans. They nod and take this in — a seamless lesson from Laurie, who is a part-time science and art teacher for Mount Sophia Academy, a middle school in Newark, DE.

A guard takes Laurie aside to point out that one of the boys is wearing a gold shirt, indicating that he's achieved a high level of good behavior. Laurie runs over to congratulate him and ask him further questions.

Aimee points out that the kids have a natural rapport with Laurie. "They love talking with her," she stated, adding that it's clear that a pet therapy animal facilitates communication. "A dog breaks down barriers and relaxes everyone. There's less pressure and stress."

Laurie agreed, recalling one day when six boys trooped into the gym. "They all looked miserable — every one of them was having a bad day," she said. "When they left, they were all smiling and laughing — they were totally different kids."

Although Laurie is a longtime PAWS volunteer (one of the first from its inception), she's only been working with Scout for the past two and a half years. They come to the detention center once a week and usually stay for 45 minutes to an hour. She said they first came to the center because they invited her. "I like kids and I had a troubled home life when I was growing up, so I understand a little of where they're coming from," she said. "When we're sitting around petting the dog, I let them know that they're young and that they have their whole lives ahead of them. They can make good choices and change their lives."

It never occurred to Laurie to be nervous or apprehensive about the kids at the detention center. "They only allow non-violent offenders to participate in pet therapy," she said, adding that each visit is supervised by Aimee and at least one guard. "We normally have anywhere from three to eight kids at a time."

When it's time to head out, the boys come over and thank both Laurie and Scout for coming in. Scout solemnly gives his paw as a final farewell to each boy. Laurie's first PAWS dog was her old golden retriever, Biscuit. When he passed away, she considered other breeds but eventually decided on another golden. She researched breeders — being careful to avoid ones that fostered inbreeding — and settled on a breeder who was focused on temperament and longevity.

Spending even five minutes with Scout is a testament to his temperament — it's impossible to imagine a sweeter or a more good-natured boy. Let's hope the longevity gene is equally as strong so he and Laurie can long continue their good work. "Seeing the kids so excited and happy — and seeing Scout so happy to be here — brings joy to my heart," Laurie said. "I love it, and Scout loves it."

PAWS for Physical and Occupational Therapy

A Husky Helps with Motivation

"Vicious" and "aggressive" are not words commonly used to describe a pet therapy animal, but these were on the cage of a three-year-old husky at a kill shelter. Fortunately, Christin Wilbert disregarded these labels and adopted Timber (so named by the rescue group because he looked like a timber wolf).

"Never once in all my time with him did I see any trace of viciousness or aggression," she said. "He was a lover — always wanting to get pets and snuggle."

As angry as that inaccurate assessment made Christin, it spurred her to explore training Timber to be a pet therapy dog. "How great would it have been to send a note back to that shelter and say: Look at what this vicious and aggressive dog is doing?"

She had heard about pet therapy and figured it would be a good fit for both Timber and herself. Even though she was working full time as an engineer at a local materials science company, she was single, had free time, and wanted to get involved in a charitable activity. "I liked the idea of volunteering and giving back but in a way that the attention wasn't on me," she explained, adding that the concept of pet therapy seemed like a no-brainer. "People who like dogs like to spend time with dogs."

Christin also surmised that she had the right dog in Timber for this work. "Timber was laid back and well-tempered," she noted. "And for him, he'd be going on car rides and getting walks, pets, and treats — all of his favorite activities."

When they first joined PAWS in the fall of 2008, Christin and Timber initially were visiting nursing homes but that was often a sad environment for them, and Christin realized that they would have to find another program. She had gone to Christiana Care Rehabilitation Services in Newark, DE, herself for physical therapy for some neck and shoulder issues and had loved the staff. "I asked the staff if they had ever considered pet therapy," she said.

As luck would have it, they had and had even been in touch with PAWS previously but had run into some logistical problems getting a team to their site. They were excited about the idea of Christin and Timber visiting on a regular basis. Instantly, it proved to be the right fit for Christin and Timber, not to mention all the dog-loving patients. "It's a fun place, with a range of ages — everyone from infants to kids to teens to adults and seniors," she said.

The center was right around the corner from where Christin lived, making it easy to go for site visits two to four days a month, typically staying for about an hour. Christin and Timber usually stuck to the same day and time slot, and this consistency allowed them to see many of the same patients again and again.

"One family was very special and they loved Timber," Christin recalled. "They would call ahead to make sure that we'd be there. They'd come early or stay late to ensure they'd cross paths with us."

Walter, a young boy with a speech and learning disability, would be in a much happier mood if Timber were there. He was always accompanied by his mother and younger sister. "When Jessica started school, I felt bad that she could no longer see Timber herself, so I'd meet up with the family at dog parks in the area."

It meant so much to that family to be able to continue their visits with Timber. "They were a great family," Christin said. "They even gave Timber Christmas presents every year. This whole experience allowed me to make so many personal connections and friendships."

Another connection was with Lisa, a young woman in a wheelchair, who came to rehab for occupational therapy. "She loved Timber and her face would light up every time she saw him," Christin said. "But then her OT schedule shifted, so she no longer got to see Timber at rehab. I found out which group home she was in so we could visit her there — she was ecstatic to visit with Timber in her home."

The company Christin worked for had a volunteer support grant program to encourage its employees to give back. Christin submitted a photo of Lisa, Timber, and herself to showcase her volunteer work. "The company made these into posters to promote the program, so I was a celebrity at work," she said, laughing at the memory. "Lisa loved the posters, too, and had one framed."

Although these were special relationships, Christin was routinely touched at how much the patients, in general, were receptive to Timber. "People love huskies," she noted, adding that they also appreciated the comic relief. "Huskies talk — sort of a funny howl — people would hear that and start to laugh."

Timber was very vocal and funny, but he was also a beautiful specimen of his breed. "He had the classic husky look with one blue eye and one brown eye and that thick perfect soft coat," Christin remembered. "He left fur everywhere he went."

Christin laughed remembering the receptionist who loved Timber. "We had to make a point to swing by and visit her every time we came in," she recalled. "She wore black pants, and these would get covered in white fur and she'd have to scotch tape it off. I'd tell her to wear white pants on our days."

The receptionist had dogs of her own at home, so Christin realized that this was her pet fix during the day. She also concluded that this was the same reason why pet therapy animals in rehab are such a success. "It's so unexpected to have a dog in that setting," she commented. "Most people think of dogs as being at home, so having one in rehab brings a sense of calm and familiarity. It makes people feel more comfortable."

That extra level of comfort played a big part in making the therapy more effective. "Having a dog there made the whole process much more enjoyable because it was a distraction from the pain and discomfort," Christin explained, adding that it was also extra motivation. "It spurred people to take a few more steps, do a few more of their exercises, and push their limits."

The staff seized on the many ways it was possible to incorporate a dog into their sessions. "They had so many great activities and games for the kids," Christin noted. "You can work on finger dexterity by picking up treats. You can improve range of arm motion by tossing treats. You can work on your ability to walk by taking a dog for a walk."

Having the physical or occupational therapy centered around an animal also helps patients overcome how slow moving and mentally exhausting therapy can be. "It's easy to think that you're not accomplishing a lot because the progress is so incremental," she said. "A dog can bring a greater sense of achievement because you walked the dog, you tossed the dog a treat."

It also helped that Timber himself was so visibly happy to take treats and to go on walks. He also loved hopping into beds to snuggle up to patients and to get combed. "He loved to be loved," Christin said.

Christin and Timber spread that love through PAWS for six years until Timber became ill and passed away at age 12. Timber was Christin's first dog to die, so, of course, his death hit her particularly hard; but she appreciated how PAWS helped her through the grieving process. "They sent me a card and ordered a memorial stone," she said, noting that Lynne of PAWS brought the stone over to her house. "That visit meant even more to me than the stone. Lynne has had dogs all of her life, and she had lost Boo Radley a few years earlier. It was like therapy to talk with her."

Now looking back, Christin is grateful for the time she had with Timber and thankful to PAWS for making his life so meaningful. "I did something great for him by rescuing him, and he did something great as a pet therapy dog," she said. "I'm so glad that he had the opportunity to do this work — it made his time here so much more valuable."

PAWS Autism Initiative Program
Leaving a Legacy

*If they can't learn the way we teach,
we teach them the way they learn.*
~ O. Ivar Lovaas

Lovaas was an applied behavioral analyst and one of the early pioneers in the field of autism. Susan Pfadt, also an applied behavioral analyst, couldn't agree more with this sentiment and is the pioneer of the PAWS Autism Initiative Program.

"A hallmark of autism is difficulty acquiring and using language," Susan explained. "Most kids on the autism spectrum struggle to learn how to communicate basic needs — yes or no, I want this, stay away."

To break through those communication barriers, Susan worked with Lynne of PAWS and Val Allen, a former PAWS staff member, to develop the PAWS Autism Initiative Program for schools. "We hooked into each student's individual education plan that maps out what skills a teacher is trying to teach a particular child," Susan explained. "We then found ways to use the pet therapy animal and the volunteer to make practicing those skills fun."

For example, when younger children are learning their colors, this lesson can be played out by letting the dog chase after different colored balls. Several different colored balls are laid out and the teacher can say, "Throw the green ball to A.G." For older children who are learning their numbers and math, they can count whiskers or use a tape measure or ruler to measure the length of the dog (or the paws or the nose).

Children on the spectrum often have trouble understanding the relationship of a word with a particular thing or activity. "To help them make that connection, we put together simple photo books about the dogs," Susan recalled. "Here is the dog getting a bath. Here is the dog going for a walk. Here is the dog going for a ride. The teacher could point to a picture and ask, 'What is A.G. doing?' These books were kept at school so they could have discussions about the dog even when the team wasn't there."

Other ongoing learning activities focused around self-care. "Most dogs like to be brushed, so we brought in a brush so the kids could brush the dogs," she said, adding that this also taught the children to identify what is used to brush hair. "We always had a napkin or paper towel with us in case the dog slobbered, the children could use that to wipe the dog's face. The teacher could then relate this to the need to sometimes wipe their own faces clean and show them how to do it."

As Susan tested out various techniques, she would meet with the teachers before and after the visit to figure out the best way to use the pet therapy animal. She also worked with the schools' speech therapists and occupational therapists. "I was often a go-between for the schools, the teachers, and the PAWS teams," she stated.

In addition, she met regularly with Lynne to fine-tune the program, assemble the necessary tools and training materials, and replicate the process for other PAWS teams. It took nearly two years to successfully develop the program, but Susan tears up a little as she explains that it was well worth the time. "Helping PAWS develop that program was a great privilege and one of the neatest experiences of my life," she said.

Since 2008, the program has grown to comprise 11 teams that work at the Brennen School (a pre-Kindergarten to 12th grade school in Newark, DE, for children on the spectrum) and its satellite programs in other elementary and middle schools. Lynne characterized Susan's contribution and participation in this program as invaluable.

"She understands the way these kids' brains work and has a clear vision about how the dogs can help connect with the kids," Lynne stated. "She has worked tirelessly guiding the pet therapy teams in their visits and has spent countless hours in the classroom. PAWS teams have gained confidence in their work thanks to Susan's calm confidence and powerful guidance."

One thing that the PAWS volunteers observed in their work in the autism program over the years was how many of the children had dogs at home. "The children themselves would tell us, or the teachers would mention it," Lynne explained, adding that this gave her the idea to help parents use their own pets to support their children. This is achieved through a class called "What Do You Do with the Dog…at Home."

"These children need structure, and schedules are a good way to achieve that," Lynne said. The care of a dog (or a cat or a rabbit) at home can easily be scheduled — at 5 p.m. — put down fresh water; at 5:15 p.m. — put out the pet's food; at 5:30 p.m. — take the animal outside or for a walk; at 7 p.m. — get ready for bed; at 7:30 p.m. — read a story to the pet.

Children on the autism spectrum are prone to meltdowns and screaming episodes, and it's often hard for the parents to get them under control. "But if the parents sense that their child is becoming overstimulated and getting more and more anxious, an animal can be a calming distraction," Lynne noted. "At those moments, the parents can say: Would you like to pet the dog? Would you like to walk the dog? Would you like to brush the dog? Would you like to take a break and watch TV with the dog?"

By stepping into the caretaking role of the family pet, this gives a child a sense of control, and it's also one less burden on the parents. "The parents are often stretched thin between support groups and counselors," Lynne said. "This relieves them of some of the pet responsibilities, while also allowing the pet to be a support to their child. It's good for the whole family."

As rewarding and satisfying as this whole experience has been, Susan is struck by how happenstance it was. Shortly after she retired from the Developmental Disability Services, an agency with the state of Delaware, she attended a PAWS charity event because a friend who had already bought the tickets fell ill and couldn't attend. "I didn't even have a dog at the time, but I went and became reacquainted with Lynne," she said, explaining that they had met years before.

One of the things that she had looked forward to in retirement was getting a dog. "I'd had cats all of my life because my work schedule didn't make it possible to have a dog — for me or the dog," she explained, noting that she choose to go with a spaniel because her late father had always had spaniels. "I knew he would be happy to know that I wound up with my own spaniel."

She found a reputable breeder for King Charles spaniels and adopted A.G. when he was 10 weeks old. The "A" is in honor of her father, Arthur. "And all pure breeds have two names, so I chose Godfrey," she said, laughing at the reference to the radio and TV personality from the 1940s and 50s (the Jimmy Kimmel of today).

At first, the intention was that A.G. would help her deal with her hearing loss. "I wear two hearing aids, but I take them out when I go to bed," Susan commented. "I wanted a dog who would be able to wake me if a fire alarm went off in my condo."

A.G. proved to be a valuable asset in that area (indeed, waking her up during a fire alarm), but she soon noticed how talented and personable he was in other ways, and this prompted her to get back in touch with PAWS. "He's sensitive to emotions," she noted. "If he hears an angry voice or someone crying — even on TV — he gets concerned."

That loving concern and happy spirit shines through in A.G.'s soft brown eyes and is matched with a teddy bear cuddliness and soft curly fur. These are an ideal set of traits for any pet therapy dog, but especially for one who is routinely visiting children who may be having a hard day. "It sometimes takes a few visits or a month or so for children on the autism spectrum to get comfortable with a dog," Susan said. "It's not uncommon for them to focus first on some physical aspect of the dog, like the ears or the tail. Then they begin to experience the dog as an individual."

A.G. is very much an individual — a little dog who is well loved and loving — who shakes hands and waves goodbye. "He is like a baby to me," Susan said, smiling at him.

Every year, the Delaware Autism Program — a statewide public school program for children and their families — hosts a big fair at the end of the school year. "The parents come with their kids, and they recognize A.G. from the cards," Susan said, referring to the "calling cards" or pet business cards. "The kids introduce A.G. — not me — to their parents."

Susan doesn't mind that little snub — she chuckles as she relays that story — because she knows the impact her work has had on children. "My life has meaning because this allows me to contribute to others," she explained. "With PAWS, there are so many ways to do that."

PAWS for Children with Special Needs

A Goldendoodle Offers a Welcome Distraction

Two curly heads, two sets of hazel eyes, two big grins. The old wives tale that dogs look like their owners is certainly true for Rhonda James and her goldendoodle (golden retriever crossed with poodle), Sienna. Rhonda is the first to admit it and even point it out: "Look at us — we're twins!" Sienna hears this familiar laugh and grins herself.

A Japanese psychologist thought there may be something to this old wives tale, so he conducted an experiment in which he asked people to match photos of people to their dogs. The experiment participants correctly matched people to their dogs 80 percent of the time, leading the psychologist to speculate that people unconsciously choose dogs who look like themselves because it fosters a sense of familiarity and comfort.

That may be the case for some pet owners, but Rhonda recalled meeting Sienna when she was a 12-week-old puppy and didn't see a strong resemblance then. "My daughter and I had driven down from New York to the breeder in New Jersey," she remembered. "It was three or four hours, and when we arrived, Sienna was the last of the litter, so we took her. She looked like a little brown teddy bear."

Even if Sienna grew to look like Rhonda, the two have always been emotionally close. "I've had other dogs throughout my life, but I am most bonded to Sienna," Rhonda stated. "As she is to me — I call myself her emotional support person."

Their close bond is a boon to both of them when they visit Rhonda's mother. "She's in a facility that offers independent living, assisted living, and a nursing home," Rhonda explained, adding that her mom is now in the nursing home. "Sienna is so good about navigating around people in walkers and putting her head in someone's lap who is sitting in a wheelchair. She remembers the people who are happy to see her. My mother is always happy to see her granddog."

This natural affinity to connect with the older people at the home sparked Rhonda's idea to train Sienna to do pet therapy. "Back in Westchester County, NY, I knew a Labradoodle who was a pet therapy dog, so I was already familiar with this concept," she said.

Four years ago when Rhonda retired from her career in human resources in the residential real estate industry and moved from New York state to Delaware, she decided it was a good time to look into pet therapy and join PAWS. "This also gave me an opportunity to meet people in this area," she said, adding that dog people are the best breed.

One site visit that allows Rhonda and Sienna to mingle with other PAWS volunteers is a week-long summer camp for children with Down syndrome, which is held in a school in Middletown, DE. "The children are preschool to elementary age," she explained, adding that she and Sienna typically go in for a two-hour visit. "The camp brings in six teams at a time so the children have a variety of dogs. This is about letting them touch and feel the dogs and get used to them — it's a sensory experience."

Rhonda's love of kids has led her to volunteer at other sites with children who have special needs. This past year, she and Sienna have visited with the children at the Early Learning Center in Newark, DE, a preschool operated by the University of Delaware. "During the school year, we went in every week for half an hour to 45 minutes," she explained, adding that the class was comprised of 18 three-year-olds with various learning and behavioral issues. "Kids are so cute and adorable at that age."

At the start of the school year, it's not uncommon for some of the youngsters to be afraid of Sienna. "She's a big dog, especially in their eyes," Rhonda stated. "Some of the kids cower and shrink away in fear."

But the teachers are understanding about this initial reaction. "For those who are afraid, we give them their space," Rhonda said. "For the rest, we bring the kids over on a one-on-one basis. Over time, this lets the others see that it's okay to pet the dog and be near her."

In addition to petting Sienna, the children take turns walking her (on the smaller double leash, while Rhonda still has Sienna on the longer leash). "I teach them how to heel, to halt — they're pleased to see that she listens to them," Rhonda said, noting that Sienna is slow and calm on these walks. "They're so proud to be able to do this — they feel like big kids."

To further the dog education process, Rhonda brings in a book for this age group, titled, *May I Pet Your Dog? The How-to Guide for Kids Meeting Dogs (and Dogs Meeting Kids)* by Stephanie Calmenson. "The teachers would read this, and it taught the kids how to approach an animal," Rhonda said. "It stresses that you have to ask the owner's permission — that you don't just run up to a dog. It also teaches them how a dog communicates with us— by its ears, tail, movements, and type of bark — and that's important as well."

Although it was a gradual progression, Rhonda said it was a wonderful experience to watch the children open up and grow. "One little boy was shy and sweet, but he was petrified of Sienna when we first arrived," she recalled. "At the end of the year, he was walking her and able to put his arms around her for a hug."

Another little girl was deathly afraid of dogs, and it was a real problem for her family when they visited cousins who had a goldendoodle. "As she got to know Sienna, she became comfortable with that family's dog, and it made their visits much easier," Rhonda remembered. "Her mother wrote me a beautiful letter thanking me."

At the end of the school year, Rhonda put together a photo album of their visits for the teachers, as well as gave each child a photo portrait of himself or herself with Sienna. Rhonda beams as she scrolls through the photos on her phone, matching the sweet, happy expressions of the children and, of course, Sienna's big smile.

But when Rhonda shifts gears to talk about their work at the Rockford Center in Newark, DE, she becomes more somber. "This is essentially a mental health unit for children with behavioral and socialization problems, as well as self-control issues," she noted, adding that they range in age from 4 to 12. "They have a variety of heavy-duty issues — everything from aggression to cases of abuse or dissociative personality disorder. Over the past three years, I've seen many of the same children return again and again."

It can be an intense environment, and Rhonda said she often feels as if she's on high alert there. "You have to have eyes in the back of your head to make sure you and your dog are safe," she said, noting that this is especially true when it comes to the older, bigger children.

Still, Rhonda looks out for Sienna, and Sienna looks out for Rhonda — both equally protective of the other. "Sienna is good about picking up on which kids are comfortable with her and not a risk — she'll be playful with them," Rhonda said. "She's more quiet and cautious with others."

Rhonda has the same go-with-the-flow temperament when it comes to the visits themselves. "We usually go once a week for an hour — sometimes less, sometimes more," she explained. "The staff is good about sensing whether a certain day will be a good day for a PAWS visit or not, depending on the overall mood or energy level of the kids that day."

And just as with the preschoolers, Rhonda gives the children at Rockford time and space to decide if they want to interact with Sienna. "I tell them: If you don't want to visit today, that's fine — maybe next time," she said, adding that most kids come around because they see the other children visiting with Sienna and want to do what their peers are doing.

Rhonda pointed out that it's also helpful to let the kids have their own one-on-one sessions with Sienna. "They can give her a treat, shake hands, pet her, or take her for a walk," she said.

While it's beneficial for these children to have that physical contact and connection with a pet therapy animal, it's even more important to have someone in their lives who is nonjudgmental. "Dogs come in with a clean slate — and even if something happens, they come back with a clean slate," Rhonda stated.

In addition, the novelty of a dog is a welcome respite. "A dog in this setting lets the children forget about everything for a little while," Rhonda said. "When we first arrive, there's always that initial jolt: There is a DOG! It's incredible to see that reaction."

Another fun activity for the children and Sienna is a special dog puzzle that Rhonda brings. "It's a wooden block puzzle with holes in the blocks to hide treats inside," she explained. "The kids put it together and then watch Sienna find the treats."

It's not uncommon for the children to talk to Rhonda about their own dogs, but she admitted that some of these stories are hard to hear. "They'll tell me things like: 'My father hit my dog' or 'My parents made me give my dog away'," she said. "So often they are coming from an abusive environment, and they're almost always going back to that environment. Some children have no family to take them."

In other cases, her heart goes out to the parents because their children may struggle with their issues all of their lives. "Some parents are doing their best, but sometimes their children have such big problems that there's a sense that they'll never truly be well," she said.

To cope with the sadness of this situation, Rhonda said she finds it helpful to talk to others. "I talk to my friends," she said. "I talk with my daughter — she has a degree in social work and is a behavioral health therapist, so she understands many of the issues these children face. I talk to Lynne [of PAWS], and she is always supportive. They all provide a good sounding board."

As challenging as these site visits can be, Rhonda said they are deeply rewarding. "Even if it's 10 minutes that these kids can take a break from their problems and enjoy the company of a dog, it makes me feel as if we've made a contribution," she said.

PAWS to DeStress
Lightening the Load

What do you get when you cross a group of stressed out humans with half a dozen dogs? A room full of smiling people and a lot of wagging tails.

This is the premise behind the PAWS to DeStress Program. In a typical destress event, six or more PAWS teams show up and provide comfort and support. During finals weeks at the University of Delaware, seven loving dogs arrived on the scene with their equally loving owners and hung out in a student lounge for two hours. This allowed the college students — usually in groups of three or more — to drop in and get a little pet therapy.

Matt Bolt, the Student Coordinator for UD's Department of Animal and Food Science, said the opportunity to come in and pet dogs is an act of decompression for the students (and for himself as well). "My dad is allergic to dogs and doesn't like dogs, so this is me having a dog vicariously," he said, adding that he also enjoys talking to the PAWS volunteers. "You get to know the owners and hear their stories, so you not only get the dogs, you get the people, too."

PAWS team Ben Franson-Wright and his mini Malinois, Sadie, each have their own interesting back stories. Ben, a UD alumni himself, had a 25-year career as an IT administrator for financial institutions, but a medical condition forced him into retirement. He adopted Sadie with the intention to train her to be a service dog to help him with his condition and his balance. She excelled as a service dog so much that Ben began to think of branching out and sharing her with others.

Fortunately for PAWS, Ben lives just down the street from PAWS volunteer Tawanda Harbison and Mr. Gibbs (her pug/beagle mix). They both convinced Ben to look into PAWS. Sadie aced her PAWS training and testing, and they've been volunteers ever since.

Sadie's story is even more compelling in that she is a Syrian refugee. A Syrian father and son team rescued 41 dogs from the war rubble in their country. They contacted the Humane Society of America, which brought all of the dogs to America; 10 of which came to Delaware. Ben shared this story with the students and quipped, "So Sadie has a valid passport, but mine is expired."

Despite her good looks and sweet nature (her Arabic name, "Basmah," means "smile"), the first two families who adopted her wound up returning her. "She's a runner," Ben said, shaking his head because he knows full well how problematic this behavior can be.

At their very first destress event at UD, Ben took Sadie outside for a little break, and she wriggled out of her harness and leash. "Ten students and I were chasing her, and she ran into the road in front of a truck," he recalled.

Even though she avoided being hit, she took off and they lost her. "I called the campus police to report a missing dog," Ben said, adding that she is microchipped, so that was a measure of comfort. "They found her — she had walked into the Barnes and Noble University Bookstore — so now she has a mug shot and a record."

This happy conclusion elicited a round of relieved laughs and extra pets for Sadie. One co-ed remarked, "She was just catching up on her reading."

Sadie listened to Ben's deep voice and hearty chortle and graciously accepted her pets (often putting a paw into someone's lap to signify that this person should hang out a little longer). If the petting stopped, Sadie would whine. Ben noticed this and would reassure the students that she's learned this is an effective way to keep the attention on her.

Gabriella, a Maltese/Yorkie mix, has learned that tail wagging that wiggles her entire eight-pound self will draw students over to her. Liza Orlando, her owner, smiled indulgently at her bowed and beloved little dog. "She is such a hambone," she said. Right on cue, Gabriella rushed over to a group of students and rolled over to receive a belly rub. "She loves being talked to."

The students obligingly talked to Gabriella, using soft voices and coos, saying things like: "She's so pretty; she's so soft; I love her bow." It's a nice break from their normal chatter of classes and finals and credits, and it's easy to see their relief and enjoyment in the simple act of indulging the little dog in some kind words and pets.

Goslar, a 10-month-old German shepherd, was also joyfully anticipating his pets and attention and not shy about offering kisses. Becky Cronin was proud of her big baby but noted that she has two other PAWS dogs at home — a corgi and another German shepherd. Although she's had dogs all of her life, her current batch of dogs are so sweet and loving that she was motivated to share them with others. A neighbor told her about PAWS, and Becky shared that her time and experiences with PAWS have literally felt like a godsend. "The year before I joined was filled with devastating events," she said. "PAWS has felt like answered prayers."

Monty, a two-year-old golden retriever and also a big kisser, was ecstatic to see a familiar college student. "She's my daughter's friend, so he recognizes her," explained Charlotte Arnold.

Barbara Cooper's son attends UD, but she said she'd just seen him over the weekend so wasn't expecting him to swing by and visit with her and Bentley, an eight-year-old chocolate Lab mix. His sleek glossy coat has splashes of white on his paws, chest, and the tip of his tail; but these markings don't detract from his look. If anything, they add an air of elegance — as if he's a Lab who accessorizes. Throughout the evening, when the stream of students thinned out, Bentley would walk over to the glass wall and peer out, wagging his tail and enticing students walking by in the hall to come in for a visit.

Barbara was equally welcoming. As the mother of a UD student herself, she has a natural in with the college students, asking them about their majors and schedule for finals, as well as about their own dogs back home.

Two other Lab mixes were in attendance — Jack, a short-furred black Lab mixed with golden retriever (also a kisser). Anthony Alioto noted that Jack eats up all the attention at these events. "He's a people person," he said. "If I take him to a dog park, he ignores the dogs and hangs out with the people."

Anthony shared that he works a psychologist but said his degree isn't necessary to discern the benefits of pet therapy. "There's no secret recipe here," he stated. "Dogs are awesome, so it's awesome to hang out with dogs."

Megan McGinness wholeheartedly agreed. Her dog, Jasmine, looks like she may have some Lab in her but Megan suspects that she's a collie/spaniel mix although she hasn't had her DNA tested. "She's half wonderful, half awesome," she said, laughing.

Like Jack, Jasmine is black and the size of smallish Lab but her coat is longer and fluffier. "She's 10 years old but thinks she's a puppy," Megan said. Her playful nature came out when a college student showed up with a skate board, and she gamely stepped onto it. The students loved playing with the dogs and petting them.

One remarked, "It's so great to be able to touch and pet these dogs — you don't see a lot of dogs on campus, and when you do, they're service animals and you can't pet them." Studies show that petting animals lowers blood pressure, reduces stress and anxiety, as well as eases loneliness. Not only that, but the tactile sensation alone — especially at a destress event — is a treat unto itself because there's such a mix of fluffy/silky/smooth/thick coats and furs.

Halfway through the evening, Ben got out some peanut butter dog treats to give to Sadie. There was an instant hush as Bentley, Jack, and Jasmine stopped socializing to sit at attention, staring intently at the treats across the room. Ben chuckled at this stereotypical Lab reaction and graciously shared the treats.

Ben mentioned that Sadie and he participate in other PAWS programs (PAWS Autism Initiative and PAWS for Physical/Occupational Therapy) and while deeply rewarding, they can be a bit intense for both of them. "The UD destress event is our destress as well," he said, noting how gentle the college students are with the dogs and that it's nice to see their empathetic side.

The students oohed and ahhed over the dogs and were sensitive about visiting all of the dogs to avoid canine hurt feelings. They also were unfailingly polite to the PAWS volunteers, answering and asking questions, and thanking the teams for coming out. Even without the spoken thank-you's, it's easy to see the non-verbal effects that the dogs have on the students. When the students first file in, they're a little frazzled and anxious, but then they plop down beside a dog and start talking and petting — almost instantly, the shoulders are relaxed, the faces soften, and then come the smiles and laughter.

The PAWS volunteers chatted and mingled with one another, with many of them noting that it's fun to be able to do a site visit with other volunteers because most of the other programs have solo teams going out to sites.

Ben commented that he and Sadie had also done a destress event for a Christiana Hospital site when it was in the midst of doing a major computer system upgrade. "I know exactly what that's like," Ben said, recalling his own IT days. "So it was really fun to be on the other side of that and be the ones making the situation lighter and happier."

PAWS volunteer Laura Dugan-Bogart also has a unique perspective on her destress events because she brings in her two-year-old German shepherd, Bane, to her own company, Discover. "I'm there as a volunteer and an employee," she said, explaining that she is a Senior Associate and serves as the program lead for the company's stress management efforts. Laura pitched Discover on the idea of a destress event at work after seeing an emotional support dog in the Phoenix office.

"I saw the calming effect this had on the entire office," she noted. "The leadership here was open to giving this a trial run."

Now more than a year later, the credit card company holds destress events once a month and several other Discover employees have become PAWS members. Laura tracks employee attendance and stress levels (always lower after a PAWS visit). "The number one feedback we get is: Can we have more of these events?" she said, adding that Bane especially loves these events because he remembers everyone. "Bane gives hugs and kisses. He has almost become the mascot for the program here and has more Facebook followers than I do."

In addition to their corporate destress events, Laura and Bane participate in pre- and post-deployment of military personnel, explaining that these are often eclectic gatherings because there's so much information to disseminate. "For pre-deployment, service members have to get their financial lives in order — everything from credit cards to mortgages to bills," she said. "With post-deployment, there are a lot of therapeutic and rehab services on hand to deal with anxiety and post-traumatic stress disorder."

To help military personnel and their families take in all of that information, free child care is available and some PAWS teams hang out in the children's room. "We sit on the floor with the kids and watch movies and play," Laura said, adding that she has an eight-year-old son, so Bane is well accustomed to children and often protective of them. "If you're in his pack, you're in his pack. He may look cool as a cucumber hanging out with the kids, but he's watching the door and making sure that everyone who comes in is supposed to be there."

A watchful dog in this setting makes both the kids and the parents feel safe and protected, and for military families especially, this must be a welcome relief after the stress of military operations and long separations.

Like Sadie and Ben, Bane quickly became a great comfort for Laura, leading to her decision to share him as a pet therapy animal. "I know that when I get home, the first thing I want to do is pet Bane and get a hug and kiss from him," she said. "PAWS allows me to share him and give back."

PAWS at Children's Hospitals
A Black Lab Lets Kids be Kids

There is no moment of higher stress or anxiety for a parent than when a child is seriously ill or injured. Brad Dunckel experienced that firsthand years ago when his eldest daughter, Emma, fell at a pool party. It appeared that she'd suffered such a serious injury that an ambulance was called and she was rushed to Nemours A.I. duPont Hospital for Children in Wilmington, DE, for evaluation.

Fortunately, Emma was not badly hurt. The only lingering side effect is that she and her sister, Maggie, (now age 13 and 9, respectively) and their father all now volunteer with their black Labrador, Luna, to help sick children and their families. Brad and Luna go to Nemours; the girls and their dad and dog go to the Ronald McDonald House of Delaware, where families can stay for free while their children are undergoing treatment.

"I was so impressed by the staff at Nemours that I wanted to volunteer in some way," Brad said. "I had read about therapy dogs and thought that could be a good way to help." He did some research and found that the dogs who volunteer at the hospital go through official pet therapy training, and Nemours directed him to PAWS.

Brad enrolled Luna into PAWS training when she was only six months old; she was fully certified two months later. Even before her training, Brad knew that she would be an ideal pet therapy dog, especially in a children's hospital. "She never jumps, never chews or nips — she's not a kisser or a licker — and she loves kids," he noted, adding that the training proved reassuring for children who might be nervous around a dog. "When I point, Luna will immediately sit or lay down."

For children who are a little shy around dogs, Brad lets them keep their distance but still encourages them to engage with Luna by tossing treats to her. "She's a Lab, so she loves food," he stated. "She catches them every time. The kids laugh and think it's funny." They also enjoy looking at her official PAWS badge that Brad admits looks very much like his work badge; he is a Senior Vice President at a major financial institution.

Brad and Luna visit Nemours every other Friday and typically stay two to three hours. From the moment they arrive, it's a flurry of pets and attention. "Even getting out of the parking lot and into the building takes us a while," Brad said, grinning at Luna's fan club. "It's a lot of stimulation for her because many times there are 10 kids petting her at once."

Children especially love how soft Luna's fur is and often tell Brad that her ears feel like those of a stuffed animal. Brad marvels at how patient Luna is with curious children who like to poke and prod. "They'll lift up her lips to look at her teeth," he said. "I show them how she has webbed feet like a duck so she can swim."

Beyond the novelty and welcome relief of a dog visit, Luna can be a real asset when it comes to medical procedures. "One day when we were volunteering, a nurse came and alerted us to the fact that a child was upset and struggling while being hooked up for a cardiac exam," Brad explained. "Luna got into the bed, and you could see on the monitor that the heart rate dropped immediately. The boy calmed down, and the nurse was able to get the test done. Luna stayed with him for 45 minutes."

Luna is also a good distraction for children when they're having blood work done. "The nurses will put the leash in a kid's hand and say: 'Keep hold of her'," Brad said, adding that he also has hold of the leash.

Luna has proven so helpful to children that it's not uncommon for parents to ask for a visit by special request if there's an upcoming stressful procedure. Brad noted that they often see the same child multiple times. "We used to see one boy in dialysis all the time, then he got his kidney transplant, so we saw him in recovery," he said, recalling another child who was there to get fitted for prosthetic legs. "Six months later, we saw her again with her new legs. She remembered Luna and walked right up to her."

Many times when Brad and Luna arrive, the child patient is asleep or too groggy to have much of an interaction. But the parents, siblings, and other family members welcome a visit. "Parents need comfort, too," Brad stated, pointing out that he and Luna often visit the parents in the waiting room before a major procedure. "They appreciate that — it helps calm them down."

Not surprisingly, the doctors and nurses at Nemours love a PAWS visit themselves. "They'll call sometimes to see if we're still around and ask if we can swing by their area for a visit before we leave," he commented.

Luna knows and loves the staff at Nemours (particularly the nurse who keeps bacon snacks at her station), but she's also good buddies with other PAWS dogs at the hospital. "She knows her friends are here even before I see them," Brad said. "Brogan, the golden retriever belonging to Pete and Diana Adamson [longtime PAWS volunteers], is her pal."

While all PAWS dogs are bathed and groomed before their site visits, a pet therapy dog who visits a hospital must be extra clean. Like a normal Lab, Luna loves hiking and running and splashing in ponds and puddles, but this comes at the price of needing regular baths. One of the categories on Luna's business card reads: Least Favorite Activity — Bath time. Brad laughs at how his water-loving dog is so resistant to warm, soapy water.

Brad's daughters helped him answer the questions on Luna's business card (they pass these out at the hospital — another big hit with the children). His favorite question and answer on her card is: Favorite Day — Today. "Luna's ability to be in the moment is perhaps her greatest quality," he said, noting that this translates over to the children. "When I bring Luna in, they just want to play with her. It takes their minds off what they're going through for a few minutes and lets them just be kids."

Brad sees this same type of reaction to his girls when they visit the Ronald McDonald House. "The kids like playing with my daughters," he said, adding that they usually visit once a month or so. "It's not even so much about Luna. They'll play the piano with Emma and Maggie. They'll play on the little jungle gym and go down the slide. It lets them be kids."

The girls both report how much they love these visits, especially seeing the impact they have on the kids and their families. "I think they appreciate that people care about them and what they are going through," Emma stated.

Maggie also loves seeing the smiles on the kids' faces when they're petting Luna. "They are happy that I brought Luna to make them happy, and they like how I am always smiling," she said.

Brad agreed that this is what being a PAWS volunteer is all about. "When I hook Luna's green leash to her collar, I tell her, 'It's time to go make smiles today'."

PAWS for Hospice
Some Final Love

In a novel by best-selling author Rachel Joyce, a queen is diagnosed with a fatal illness and goes into a hospice run by nuns and announces, "I am here to die." The Sister in charge replies, "You are here to live until you die. There is a significant difference."

Lynne of PAWS would agree with this sentiment. "Hospice visits are sweet and precious because you know the person's days are numbered," she said, explaining that hospice care is typically reserved for those who are expected to die within six months or less. "But the focus should be on the life that's left."

A pet therapy visit can go a long way to inject life and comfort into those final days, weeks, or months. "With hospice visits, almost always the animal is in the bed for hugging and petting," Lynne noted. "It's all about the physical connection to another being."

If it's not possible to accommodate a dog (or a cat or rabbit) into someone's bed, it's still possible for the dog to stand beside the bed to receive a pet or to lick a hand. "That type of contact is better than what most of the humans can provide," Lynne said.

But PAWS human volunteers can still provide a valuable service to hospice patients. "We can listen," Lynne said, adding that telling and retelling stories can often be part of the dying process. "It's sort of like a final purging. Their family has heard these stories before, but the PAWS volunteers have not, so they can listen and let people tell their stories one more time."

With other hospice patients, it's not uncommon for them not to talk at all. "Sometimes they're conserving their energy to talk to family or they're going inward," Lynne noted, adding that PAWS volunteers in this program get special hospice training. "It's important to understand what's going on with hospice patients, so we can be responsive to their needs."

In many cases, a PAWS visit brings happy memories for the patients. "They may recall their childhood pet and playing with their siblings and the dog in the backyard," Lynne said. "What a sweet remembrance for them."

In some hospice settings, there may be many relatives gathered around the patient; and this stage of grief can be unsettling and difficult. "Often, the families are waiting for the person to move, to wake up, to resurrect, or to die," Lynne said. "To bring a dog into this situation makes things a little more normal and stable."

Family members can pet the dog, talk about the dog, and share stories about their dogs. "It's a welcome distraction and gives them something to do," Lynne noted, recalling one hospice visit with an Asian family.

"There were more than a dozen family members there, and they were all just standing around while the grandfather slept," she said. "Eventually, the grandfather stirred and was nudged by the dog. He woke up, looked at the dog, and smiled. This let them all know that he was still in there and that they could still talk to him and say goodbye."

Most PAWS volunteers in the hospice program go out on visits once a week (sometimes more) and typically stay for an hour or so. "The length of the visit depends on whether the patient is awake and how long the patient stays awake," Lynne explained, adding that sometimes volunteers arrive at a hospice facility and walk around to see who is up and who would welcome a visit. "In other cases, the staff at a nursing home or facility will assign a specific patient to a volunteer for a visit."

The most personal hospice visit for Lynne was one for her father-in-law. "He was semi-conscious and in bed," she remembered. "Suddenly, his breathing changed. My husband leaned forward and told him that he loved him and it was okay to go. Two seconds later, he stopped breathing and was gone. It was a gift to be there to witness his passing and to be with him in his final hour."

Surprisingly, Lynne did not have any of her golden retrievers in attendance. "Of course, if we'd had one of our dogs there, that dog would have comforted us in that moment," Lynne stated, adding that this has been the case in other hospice deaths. "The pet therapy animals provide a real service to everyone in this situation."

Considering all of PAWS programs, Lynne is struck by the age span that the organization reaches. "We visit everyone from toddlers all the way through to the end of life — and connecting with everyone in between," Lynne said.

PAWS by Special Request
Granting Wishes

Despite all the specialized programs that PAWS offers, there are still situations that fall outside those areas or the timing dictates a special request or perhaps the need for a particular type of pet or even a certain breed. "Sometimes people call up and say: 'I need a basset hound'," explained Lynne of PAWS.

A memorable special request for Lynne came from parents of a gravely ill little girl. "They called and said they needed a cat to come to their house within 24 hours," Lynne said, speculating that the child was between hospital visits. "Given the time line, I ran home and got my cat, Lacie."

Lacie, a big, beautiful long-haired black and white tuxedo cat, was 23 years old at the time, and she perfectly fit the bill. "That little girl was thrilled from the moment she set eyes on her," Lynne stated, adding that even though she was an elderly cat, her motor was in good working order. "She purred as she took her up to her bedroom, she purred as she showed her her dollhouse, she purred as she showed her her little car."

"It was a real gift to the parents to be able to fulfill this wish for their little girl," Lynne recalled. "They had tears in their eyes as stood there watching the interaction between their child and the cat. Lacie, who responded easily to petting and cuddling, purred up a storm and was happy to be there — she was a dream come true. They couldn't have had this reaction from a stuffed animal — it had to be a real live cat." The parents were beyond grateful to Lynne, Lacie, and PAWS.

A more common special request comes from older couples who have had dogs all of their lives, but when their last old dog passes away, they feel they are too old to adopt again. "In those cases, we can arrange a PAWS visit every week or every few weeks so they still get some dog time," Lynne explained.

When Jocelyn Langrehr first looked into joining PAWS two years ago with her cat, Shadow, she wasn't sure if he would be a good fit. "But the PAWS staff met with us at their offices for our training, and they assured me that he would be a natural," she recalled, thanking them for what proved to be a correct assessment.

At first glance, Shadow is a magnificent cat — a deep all over gray (even his broad lion-like nose is gray) with a luxurious coat. When happy, he winces his eyes in pleasure. "We suspect he's part Russian blue," Jocelyn said, adding that his thick fur likely helped him survive his first winter.

Jocelyn recounted that a cat rescue group found him hurt and hungry next to a dumpster during a very cold February four years before. They estimated he was only six months old at the time. The group spayed him and then fostered him out to two homes. Jocelyn had tracked his progress, and when the last foster home didn't work out, she adopted him. Shadow was a welcome addition to her home of five cats, and under Jocelyn's care and feeding, he has grown to be an 18-pound cat.

His old injuries left him partially deaf and blind in one eye; but, surprisingly, these make him a better therapy cat. "Because he's down two senses, the sense of touch is really important to him," she said, adding that their normal nursing home visits are a tactile treat for him. "He loves the carpeting in the hallway, and, of course, he loves the pillows and blankets on the residents' beds. He gets in there and cuddles up and gets some pets and falls asleep in total bliss."

Jocelyn's favorite person to visit at the nursing home is the former cat lady of the neighborhood. "She had cats herself and fed and looked after feral cats in the area, but then she became too old to live on her own and had to go to a nursing home. It's a real comfort to her to have a cat brought in for a personalized visit."

Many of the other nursing home residents also appreciate a cat visit. "For many older people, the last pet they had before going to a nursing home was a cat, so it's especially nice for them to have a cat visit," stated PAWS volunteer Sue Soder. "They enjoy visits from the PAWS dogs, but we get a lot of requests for cats. I think a cat makes it feel more like home."

Jocelyn noted that she's always surprised how animated the residents become when they first set eyes on Shadow. "They start telling me about their former pets. Even the folks with dementia who aren't normally big talkers will share their stories."

Jocelyn serves as Deputy Director for the Division of Vocational Rehabilitation for Delaware's Department of Labor. When the agency held a spa day for employees, management thought it would be fun to include therapy dogs from PAWS, but soon the special request came in for a cat, so Jocelyn brought in Shadow. "We set him up away from the dogs in his own area," she explained, noting that their nursing home visits are normally only an hour or two. "But he was there at the office the full day — I brought in a portable kitty litter box — and he did great."

After their pampering and spa treatments, the relaxed employees turned their attention on Shadow. He luxuriated in all the pets and was the picture of contentment, making everyone who touched him even more relaxed and happy. "The feedback was outstanding," Joceyln said. "The biggest response was: When can we do this again?"

Like Jocelyn and Shadow — Megan O'Donnell, a personal trainer, and her therapy rabbit, Edward — also normally visit nursing homes. And like Jocelyn and Shadow, one of them has a harrowing back story, but it's not Edward. Before Megan adopted him four years ago, he was a classroom bunny, so she knew that he was accustomed to being petted and handled. And she knew what a comfort he was in times of stress because he'd helped her deal with the aftermath of the mass shooting in Las Vegas in 2017. "After surviving that, I just really wanted to put some good back into the world," Megan stated. "I felt like I had earned this second chance, and I wanted to make it a good one. Working with animals and the community — and specifically, the elderly — just felt right."

Like all PAWS therapy animals, Edward wears a harness and is on a leash. "We do our best to get down to people on their level whether they're in chairs, wheelchairs, or beds," Megan explained. "He's happy to sit with people — either in bed, on laps, or in arms."

In addition to the nursing home, Megan and Edward attend community events and have also participated in mental health support groups and a few military deployments. They took time out of their busy schedules to pay a special request visit to the preschool class at Mount Aviat Academy, a private Catholic school in Childs, MD.

The children were overjoyed to meet Edward. Their eyes lit up, and they literally squealed in delight. As a lionhead rabbit, he has the characteristic thick mane around his neck and his tawny coloring is also lion-like. He's so big and fluffy that it's almost hard to believe he's a real rabbit versus a stuffed toy. Sister Joseph Margaret, the preschool teacher, had the children sit in a circle on the floor, and Megan put Edward in the center of the circle, and he hopped in different directions so everyone had a chance to pet him. Even though they were still happy and excited to have a visit from a rabbit, the children soon calmed down and were quiet and gentle as they stroked his fur.

The children asked a lot of questions, and Megan did her best to answer all of them. Does he eat carrots? (Yes, but mostly rabbit pellets.) Does he get along with dogs? (Yes, he lives with a chocolate Lab.) Does he like other rabbits? (Not sure.) Where does he live? (At the house in a large indoor crate.)

When the children waved and said goodbye to Edward, Megan explained that they were on their way for another special request visit to the nursing home where they normally go. "A family friend was coming for a visit that day and she knew that the resident loved animals, so she reached out and requested a therapy animal be there during her visit," she explained. "Edward and I were happy to answer the call."

They were even happier to realize that it would be a group visit because when Megan and Edward arrived, the resident was attending a birthday party. "For sure, she lit up," Megan said. "I actually see her often on our regular visits, and she always loves Edward. She held him for a bit, and then he made his rounds around the room with the other birthday celebrants and even two of the care workers. It was a great experience."

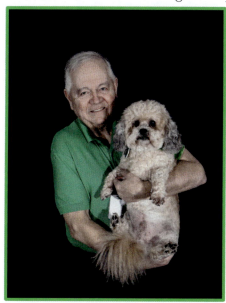

For John Weber and Gizmo, his 11-year-old poodle/shih tzu mix, they tend to have special preferences versus special requests. "Sometimes large dogs can be intimidating, especially for children," John stated. "When we first started coming to the library for PAWS for Reading, I remember a girl who was happy to see that there was a little dog available."

They also volunteer at the emergency room at Nemours A. I. duPont Hospital for Children, and Gizmo's size is an asset there as well. "Because he's a small dog, it's easy to lift him and put him into bed with a child," John explained, adding that parents are so grateful that they often ask for further information about PAWS. "I always have brochures on hand to pass out to let people learn more about the organization."

John himself learned about PAWS at a community event at a local Boscov's five years ago. Knowing what a friendly and sociable dog he had in Gizmo, he knew this would be a good fit. "My wife and I adopted him from a shelter when he was two, and that first week that we had him, we had a dinner party and he was the life of the party," he said, smiling at the memory. As a full-time Safety Officer for DART (Delaware Area Regional Transit), John said he appreciates that PAWS offers its volunteers the flexibility to make visits during evening and weekend hours.

At a recent PAWS for Reading visit, children flocked to the team. John, a granddad of eight and great-granddad of one, had spread out a bright red fleece blanket and smiled when youngsters approached with their books. Gizmo was equally welcoming, wagging his tail and eager to meet new friends. As each child read, Gizmo settled in and lay down (back legs splayed out), happy to take pets from John or toddler siblings. When one little girl stopped at each page to show him the picture book, Gizmo sat at attention. At the end of each book reading, Gizmo rolled over on his back to get some belly rubs. His soft curly fur is a natural magnet.

One little boy, who was quiet and shy when he first sat down on the blanket, quickly read through his book. John complimented him on his reading and stamped his card (five stamps and the children earn a tee shirt). Both of these got a big smile out of the boy, who then sat back on his heels and seemed more at ease now that his reading assignment was complete and had gone well. Having Gizmo beside him on the blanket added to his relief. He grinned at the little dog and told John, "I want to tickle him." That's one special request that's easy to accommodate.

PAWS at Peace
Saying Goodbye

It's been said that to adopt a pet is to initiate a countdown to sorrow. Most animal lovers expect to outlive their pets and know that the day will come when they will have to say goodbye. Grief over the loss of an animal is hard on all pet owners, but it often cuts deeper for PAWS members.

Many joined PAWS out of a profound love of their pet and their desire to share their pet with others. Once they are trained and out in the community going on regular site visits, the bond between the person and the animal naturally gets deeper and stronger because they are working together with a shared purpose. PAWS members have seen firsthand the comfort and joy that their pets have brought to people in the community. They've seen how their animals instinctively know who to go to, who needs a paw to hold, who needs a calming presence. They've seen the smiles and basked in the gratitude of those they've visited. When therapy pets pass away, it's not just a personal loss for their owners, but a greater loss to the community.

To comfort and support its members during this hard time, the entire PAWS staff springs into action as soon as it gets word of a pet death. "Laura orders flowers, and Sammy sends a card and updates the database," explained Lynne of PAWS, adding that her role is to immediately call the member. "This is not a rote `sorry for your loss' type of call. We talk about the pet and about the life and service of that animal."

After the call, Lynne follows up with an email to go over all the ways that PAWS offers additional support. For starters, there are several physical mementos — a memory stone with an inscription chosen by the member; a keepsake charm handcrafted by PAWS member Cindy Baker; an engraved plate to be added to the PAWS Old Friends Memorial Plaque, which is in the office lobby. Lynne will personally deliver these keepsakes if the member would like to have a visit to talk about the pet, look at photos, and further reminisce.

In addition, PAWS writes an obituary that it runs in its newsletter. PAWS also offers its members the option to get grief counseling with Diane Mayer, a professional bereavement counselor. "She lives on a beautiful farm in Avondale, PA, and she invites her clients to walk and talk about their pets," Lynne noted. "She encourages people to celebrate the life of the animal."

This outpouring of care and concern is central to PAWS. "Pets are what PAWS is all about," Lynne stated. "This is about acknowledging that and recognizing their importance and their service. People are bereft, and all the things we offer help with closure." All of the PAWS at Peace offerings are underwritten by a generous member who feels strongly about the need to acknowledge the importance of therapy pets.

Longtime PAWS members, Penny and Greg Taylor, recently suffered the loss of Trinity Grace, their beloved English golden retriever. Penny had first learned of PAWS at a Newark Community Day, when she was a newly retired nurse and Trinity was two. She remembered thinking that this would be a rewarding way to spend time with her dog and give back to the community at the same time.

Over their decade-long run at PAWS, they visited nursing homes, hospitals, and participated in the PAWS for Reading program and the Trauma Support program. Trinity received her Master's Certification, the highest level of certification available through PAWS.

Greg recalled Trinity's soft, cream-colored coat, while Penny remembered her empathetic nature. "She sensed who needed her, and she would tug on her leash to get me to take her to certain people," she said, adding that once they got closer, Trinity would lean into people.

Both of the Taylors shared how much they appreciated all the love and support from Lynne and the staff at PAWS. "When a pet dies, a lot of people don't get it — it's like losing a child," Penny said. "If you don't have animals, you don't understand."

Penny said a lot of people think it's okay to send condolences over Facebook, but the cards and flowers mean so much more.

"I used to do the Facebook thing myself, but now I try to be a little more sensitive and give a little more than is expected," Penny said.

Greg commented that many people just don't know what to do when someone's pet dies. "But we were both pleasantly surprised at all the things that PAWS did," he said.

"It did help," Penny stated. "We had 13 beautiful years with her, and I'm sure she is continuing her therapy work in Heaven. Once I've healed enough, I'll get another golden and be back at PAWS."

Lynne commented that while she's always happy to see former members open their hearts and homes to another pet and come back to PAWS, it's still important that PAWS honor and remember the therapy animals and their years of service. "We want our members to know how seriously we take them and their pets, even if they won't be returning," she stated. "And we want all of our members to know that we will be there for them in their time of sorrow."

Other PAWS members shared how much that love and support meant to them. When Nancy Shurkoff lost Sawyer, her golden retriever, she was overwhelmed with grief but also with the outpouring of love and support from PAWS. "Sawyer was very, very special to us — he was my everything," she said. "I appreciate your call, your concern, and your kindness. Thank you, Lynne, for creating PAWS and for allowing us to be part of and to experience all the wonderful aspects of PAWS. It has honestly changed my life for the better, and it was one of the best and most rewarding and enlightening times of my life."

Two other PAWS members were especially thankful for their sympathy flowers. When Nancy Frey's black Labrador, Stella, passed away, she wrote: "Thank you so very much for such a lovely surprise this morning. I was just thinking about my girl today and missing her a lot as usual. Your thoughtfulness and kindness mean so much to me."

Kate Becker was also moved by her bouquet of colorful flowers following the loss of her German shepherd, Eliza. "That was so kind of PAWS," she said. "Eliza's time was too short on this earth, but I am doing better every day. You and the PAWS family are wonderful, caring, and compassionate friends."

PAWS Training
A Culture of Caring

Kind — Compassionate — Light-hearted — Inclusive
Flexible — Problem-solving — Supportive

These are a handful of "culture words" for PAWS for People — important values that the organization hopes to project in all of its interactions in the community. They are integral to PAWS training and everything PAWS does. These values are all on display when potential teams — owners and pets — arrive for their volunteer training session.

Kind/Compassionate

Lynne of PAWS — along with trainers/PAWS volunteers Luann D'Agostino, Susan Good, and Marilyn Huebner — smiled and greeted the teams. They thanked everyone for coming in; they loved on the dogs; and they gave equal attention and reassurance to the owners. This happy, warm welcome set the tone for the evening and helped to allay anxieties.

"When the teams first come in, they're often a little nervous and worried if their pets will pass our certification test," Lynne said, explaining that the testing covers proficiency with basic dog obedience commands, as well as the pet's general behavior and, most importantly, the relationship between the pet and the owner. (Cats and rabbits are assessed for sociability and typically come to the PAWS offices separately.)

Problem-solving

If a dog struggles with one or two of the commands, the trainers work one-on-one with the dog and owner to master those moves. They also pass out instruction sheets with further guidance and tips to help the teams work on these at home. Teams are retested at the second training session (or at a later date) to make sure they can successfully perform all of the commands.

Once the pets have successfully received their training, the teams move to the next step to learn the in's and out's of site visits. The trainers go over what to pack, what to watch out for at a site, commendable pet etiquette, and how to handle situations that will probably come up during real visits. This includes things like dealing with a cranky person, handling someone who is allergic or afraid of animals, and reading body language and listening attentively to what is being said.

Moira Stephan, PAWS Training Director, went over how to handle common scenarios that PAWS volunteers may encounter. "What if somebody asks you for a glass of water?" she asked, adding that this may seem like a harmless request. "But what if that person is not allowed liquids at that time? You can pass along the request to staff or to a nurse."

To avoid running into privacy issues, Luann pointed out that PAWS volunteers must maintain confidentiality. "If you see someone you know at a site — say at a hospital or at a rehab facility — you cannot share that information with anyone else," she stated. "Even if a neighbor is wondering how so-and-so is doing, you don't pass along that you visited or saw that person at the site."

Light-hearted

Luann laughed when she explained that PAWS visits are often lopsided. "Some people may ignore your pet but want to talk to you," she noted. "Some people don't care about you and are only focused on the pet. Either way is fine — you are there to go in and make magic."

Marilyn pointed out that the magic starts instantly. "As soon as you put on the PAWS leash, you're on the clock," she said. "You may meet people in the parking lot who want to pet your dog, that's fine. In the lobby, that's fine. In the elevator, that's fine. The staff at the site may want a visit, that's fine. It may take you an hour to get to the people you're visiting that day, but this is all part of the experience."

Supportive

To help new volunteers get started, Moira pointed out that PAWS has more than 20 programs that encompass nearly 200 sites. "We love it when our volunteers tell us that they're open to going anywhere," she said, but added that the staff will help new teams figure out what type of program or sites they might like. "If you already visit one of our sites and want to go there, that's great. If you visit a site that PAWS doesn't go to, talk to us and maybe we'll be able to arrange site visits there."

New teams are accompanied by a PAWS staff person or an experienced volunteer on their first site visits. "This helps everyone remember the rules and makes the visit go smoother," Moira said, noting that teams don't have to stick with their original sites. "You might find that your dog is at the nursing home and would rather be around children. That's fine — we're flexible."

Flexible

Longtime PAWS volunteers Thom and Val Rowan said they appreciate the organization's flexibility, especially as their chocolate Lab, Sophie, has aged. "When we first joined PAWS 10 years ago, we were going to two elder care sites," Thom said. "Then about five years ago, we started going to Nemours A.I. duPont Hospital for Children, and we were there for three years."

But then Sophie tore a ligament in her knee and had to have surgery. In addition, she is prone to arthritis, and both of these proved hard in the hospital setting with slippery floors. "Sophie lies down when people pet her, and she was really struggling to get up and back on her feet," Thom explained. "We didn't want her to slip and get hurt, and PAWS is very clear that you are the advocate for your dog. They were understanding when we retired her from the hospital."

Now, Sophie is back to elder care and also is a substitute in the PAWS for Reading Program at a local library.

Inclusive

Another team that appreciates that fact that PAWS is inclusive is Anne Dunlap and her black Labrador, Gizmo. Twenty years ago when Anne was 18, she was in serious car accident that left her with mobility issues and memory loss. In 2010, Gizmo came to her through Canine Partners for Life as a service dog to alert her to impending seizures. Having seen the benefits of pet therapy firsthand, Anne wanted to share Gizmo with others. When she and her mother, Debbie, read about PAWS in the newspaper, they looked into becoming volunteers.

"Gizmo is so happy and energetic and he's such a people dog, it didn't seem right for him to just be sitting at home as a service dog," Anne said.

Anne has a rotating crew of personal assistants to help her with daily living tasks, and they attend PAWS training so they can go on site visits with Anne and Gizmo. "PAWS lets us have one membership that covers three personal assistants," Debbie stated, adding that she is grateful that Lynne recognized that Anne could still give back to the community. "It sends an important message that says: Yes, accidents happen, but it's not stopping us — we're still out there helping others."

Anne and Gizmo visit weekly with nursing home residents; they also attend PAWS to DeStress events at the University of Delaware. (Debbie and Gizmo also participated in the PAWS for Reading Program, but now that Gizmo is older and has arthritis, he has retired from this program.) Debbie commented that PAWS documentation makes it easy for people with memory issues to remember all the things that they should bring on a site visit, as well as easy to log in the volunteer hours (PAWS asks its volunteers to commit to two site visits a month). "Lynne is one smart lady — she set up PAWS to be a success," she said.

Lynne agreed that she loves to see her teams succeed and commented that her favorite part of volunteer training is graduation. "The teams come up and get their certificates and gift bags," she said, explaining that these are filled with pet supplies and a gift certificate for PAWS therapy team tee shirts and other PAWS Wear. "They're so happy and proud of their pets (and secretly of themselves). Getting through orientation, testing, and training takes time and commitment from our teams — not to mention a great deal of loving care and patience from the trainers. In the end, our newcomers are full members of PAWS and prepared to bring comfort and joy to the community. We're as happy as they are!"

Conclusion

Kind readers, I've written this conclusion several times; and, each time, I felt that the words didn't match the feelings and stories you have just read in this book. I couldn't find the right words to end this tour through PAWS, meeting our people and our pets, and learning about the impact that pet therapy has on everyone involved. And then I realized why.

There is no conclusion to the PAWS for People story — no ending in sight. We're simply not finished — not even close. PAWS is always moving forward, always responding to the changing needs of our community, always growing.

Each day, we receive two to three requests from new sites asking for our services. We wish we could answer each one with a "YES, we'll be there" because we'd like to help everyone who needs us. We train between 20 to 25 people every month — we're lucky that so many come to us trusting we will train them well and match them with the right program and sites where they can make a distinct difference in other people's lives. We support and encourage everyone with a gentle, affectionate pet to try pet therapy to see if it's the right fit for them — and most often it is. We create classes to teach our teams about the different groups of people they'll be visiting and educate them about each particular demographic so they have a better understanding of the specific needs and behaviors of the people they'll be encountering. That, in turn, makes their visits better and more effective.

When we accompany a new team on their first visit, we always ask afterwards: "How was it? Were you and your pet comfortable? Was this what you were hoping for?" And what we most often hear is the reply I always hope we'll get back: "It was amazing. This is even better than I thought it would be. I think I got more out of this visit than the folks we spent time with. Is that okay?" It is definitely okay. It's part of the deeper impact of pet therapy. Everybody benefits, everybody's life is improved.

PAWS for People has so much more to do — more teams to train, more people to reach, more healing to offer — we're looking forward to doing all that and more. And, even though we're still growing, we're grateful and proud of what PAWS has become. Boo would be, too.

To Learn More About PAWS…

Go to www.pawsforpeople.org

If you would like to volunteer with your gentle, affectionate dog, cat, or bunny; please click "Volunteer" on the top bar of the home page, answer some questions about your pet, and fill out and submit the online application. A PAWS staff member will contact you to conduct a short phone interview and let you know when the next training sessions will be held in your area.

Once you and your pet have successfully completed your training, a staff member or a long-time PAWS volunteer will accompany you on your first site visit. Staff members are always available to answer questions or concerns as they arise.

Opportunities to volunteer without a pet are also available (see website for more information); donations are gratefully accepted.

Also, please consider posting a recommendation or review of this book on social media and/or on Amazon.com.

A previous picture book by Lynne Robinson, *PAWS Therapy Dogs*, is available for purchase at the PAWS offices.

Acknowledgments

PAWS for People wishes to thank the thousands of people who have welcomed our visits and shared with us that our therapy pets have "made their day." It's heartening to know that people have been touched in a positive way. When they tell us things like: "You made all the difference" and "Your dog saved my life," we know that we're having a positive impact in a world where more love and acceptance and magical moments are needed. These heartwarming messages are verbal proof that pet therapy is an effective way of helping someone heal.

We thank our current volunteers (and those who have been part of PAWS for People along the way) who venture out into the community every day, sharing their time and their pets to bring comfort and joy to others. We thank our members who volunteer their time and talents at the office and who work on special projects throughout the year. We are graced with so many giving people who love the concept of pet therapy and work hard to support PAWS in every way possible.

While Lynne is grateful for all of the PAWS members and is dear friends with many of them, she has a special place in her heart for those who have gone above and beyond the norm to assist in making PAWS what it is today. Heartfelt thanks to Special Advisor Alan Burkhard, whose business expertise has kept PAWS on a straight course. His support and his friendship are deeply appreciated. Thanks to our many staff members and interns who have worked tirelessly to keep PAWS running. Thanks to our board members who have taken on special responsibilities to keep PAWS fiscally stable. And most importantly, thanks go to Winston Robinson, the most supportive husband ever, and Wendy Lewis, not only a supportive daughter but also a key player in the inner workings of PAWS.

Lynne also thanks Rachel Brown, the freelance writer and editor for this project, who was delighted to meet and interview all of the teams, making this book possible from start to finish. Rachel wishes to thank Janice Baldwin-Hench and Denise Marotta Lopes, two talented writers who graciously allowed her to use some of their interviews and stories from the teams.

Most of all, our hearts and appreciation go out to our awesome therapy pets who do their jobs with a happy smile, a bouncy step, and their innate intuition that leads them to seek out the hurt and lonely to provide much needed companionship and one-on-one attention. They are the bridge by which we humans can be part of the magic.

And finally, Lynne thanks Boo Radley for coming into her life and sharing his uncanny knack for looking into people's eyes and letting them know through a gentle lean and a healing presence that everything was going to be all right.

About the Authors

Lynne Robinson is the Executive Director of PAWS for People, a nonprofit volunteer pet therapy organization she founded in 2005. When she retired after 23 years as an English teacher, Lynne looked for meaningful volunteer work but had difficulty finding the right fit. A lifelong animal lover and dog owner, she rescued a bedraggled and neglected golden retriever and almost instantly realized that she had a very special dog. He was uniquely in tune with others and could convey a sense of comfort and peace. Lynne's desire to share him with others is what launched PAWS. Her teaching background reinforced the need to train volunteers for programs that are individually tailored to address the emotional, mental, and physical wellbeing of pet therapy recipients. Lynne understood that the experience had to be positive for the recipients but also for the human volunteers and their therapy animals.

PAWS for People has grown to be the largest pet therapy organization in the Mid-Atlantic region with more than 650 active therapy teams who visit nearly 200 sites throughout Delaware, Pennsylvania, New Jersey, and Maryland. While Lynne is busy overseeing PAWS as a whole and working with the volunteer teams, she continues to pilot new programs and still goes out on site visits every week with two of her goldens, Tory and Joy, and her cat, Moxie.

Rachel Brown is a freelance writer with more than 25 years' experience. She lives in Newark, DE, with her husband, Tom; her son, Joe; and her emotional support staff, consisting of a beagle and two cats.

Made in the USA
Middletown, DE
05 December 2019